By Charles G. Fuller

-Contributing Author to:

-"The Priority of Prayer", *Faithful to the Lord*, compiled by E. Stanley Williamson, Nashville: Broadman Press, 1973, p. 45

-"The Language of Sorrow", *For Those Who Grieve*, compiled by R. Earl Allen, Nashville, Broadman Press, 1978, p. 53

-"The Ties that Bind", *Waiting in the Wings*, compiled by Porter Routh, Nashville, Broadman Press, 1978, p. 155

-"Barren Branches", *Southern Baptist Preaching Today*, compiled by R. Earl Allen and Joel Gregory, Nashville, Broadman Press, 1987, p. 103

-"Partakers of Christ", *Discipleship Sermons*, compiled by Roy Edgemon and William Stephens, Nashville, Broadman Press, 1990, p. 45

-"Ceremony 7", *The Wedding Collection*, compiled by Morris H. Chapman, Nashville, Broadman Press, 1991, p. 74

-"Preaching and Education" *Handbook for Contemporary Preaching*, compiled by Michael Duduit, Nashville, Broadman Press, 1992, p. 464

-"How To Think Like a Soul Winner", *Soul Winning Motivational Sermons*, compiled by Jack R. Smith, North American Mission Board, 1994, p. 57

-"Ten Commandments for Christian Citizens", *Christians in the Public Square: Faith in Practice?*, Nashville, ERLC Publications, 1996, p. 23

Author:
Give Him Time, Bloomington, Crossbooks Publishing, 2009

The Awesome Power of the Tongue

Dr. Charles Fuller

WestBow
PRESS
A DIVISION OF THOMAS NELSON

Copyright © 2012 by Dr. Charles Fuller.

All rights reserved. No part of this book may be used or reproduced by any means, graphic, electronic, or mechanical, including photocopying, recording, taping or by any information storage retrieval system without the written permission of the publisher except in the case of brief quotations embodied in critical articles and reviews.

All Scripture quotations, unless otherwise indicated, are taken from the New American Standard Bible, (NAS, NASB) Copyright 1998 by the Lockman Foundation, Foundation Publications, Inc., Anaheim, California.

Other Scripture references are from the following sources:

The Message, Eugene H. Peterson, NavPress Publishing Group, 1993

The Holy Bible, King James Version, (KJV), Zondervan Publishing

WestBow Press books may be ordered through booksellers or by contacting:

WestBow Press
A Division of Thomas Nelson
1663 Liberty Drive
Bloomington, IN 47403
www.westbowpress.com
1-(866) 928-1240

Because of the dynamic nature of the Internet, any web addresses or links contained in this book may have changed since publication and may no longer be valid. The views expressed in this work are solely those of the author and do not necessarily reflect the views of the publisher, and the publisher hereby disclaims any responsibility for them.

Any people depicted in stock imagery provided by Thinkstock are models, and such images are being used for illustrative purposes only.

Certain stock imagery © Thinkstock.

ISBN: 978-1-4497-6987-1 (hc)
ISBN: 978-1-4497-6986-4 (sc)
ISBN: 978-1-4497-6985-7 (e)

Library of Congress Control Number: 2012918289

Printed in the United States of America

WestBow Press rev. date: 10/15/2012

Contents

Acknowledgements 7
Foreword 9
Preface: Awesome is the Word 11
The Worshipping Tongue 13
The Truthful Tongue 29
The Forgiving Tongue 45
The Imploring Tongue 59
The Acid Tongue 75
The Positive Tongue 87
The Encouraging Tongue 103
The Silent Tongue 117
The Household Tongue 133
The Witnessing Tongue 147
The Tongue and the Heart 163
Conclusion: A War of Words 177

Acknowledgements

Special Thanks…

To Carol, my wife and partner in ministry, who continues to encourage me to extend my preaching experience of fifty years through writing. This book owes its existence to the investment of many hours of her time.

To Robin Amstutz, who added personal interest to her role of transcriber and proof reader. Her editorial contributions were both welcome and timely.

To Jonathan McGraw, graphic artist, who captured the message of the book in his design of the front cover.

To Nancy Prillaman, my secretary, who remains an encourager and who has devoted herself to the author's outreach ministries of God's Time, Inc.

And to Jerald R. White, Jr., author in his own right and brother in the ministry for over 50 years, for his forceful and gracious Foreword.

Foreword

Sobering words came from the mouth of the Lord Jesus Christ, "I tell you, on the day of judgment people will give account for every careless word they speak, for by your words you will be justified, and by your words you will be condemned" (Matthew 12:36-37, ESV). All that Jesus spoke was truth, but when He said, "I tell you," it is like He was speaking in capital letters. "Pay attention and listen carefully" was clearly implied.

It has been said that saints of "yesteryear" only had two dates on their calendar--- TODAY and THAT DAY. Everything I say and do today should be with a view to that day when I will stand before my Creator and Judge to give an account of the deeds (and words) done in the body (2 Corinthians 5:10). Grasping this truth should have a dramatic effect on how we live and speak today. Taking it seriously will cause restraint of careless words and encourage using kind words.

The devil's words slander, oppress and destroy. Jesus' words heal, encourage and deliver. He said, "The words that I have spoken to you are spirit and life" (John 6:63, ESV). The question is, which one do you and I want to be like---the evil one or the Lord Jesus?

To become like Jesus means to overflow with God's love from one's heart so that words spoken are rooted in agape love, not sinful selfishness.

I have known Charles Fuller for fifty-four years and served with him on his church staff in both of his pastorates while I was in college and seminary. My early mentor and dear friend has written a timely and much needed book on the incredible power of the tongue. In his usual simple, readable, and practical style he lays out for us wise instructions from God's Word on the use of this small organ that is inseparably bound to one's heart (Matthew 12:34). The tongue, like a ship's rudder, controls the direction of your life, but it is impossible to bridle this tiny instrument without being under the all-powerful control of the Holy Spirit.

The Awesome Power of the Tongue will challenge, encourage and instruct you on how to use your tongue so that you will not be ashamed on THAT DAY.

Jerald (Jerry) R. White, Jr.

Preface

Awesome is the Word

Boasting mighty things, the tongue can verbalize blessing and cursing, the truth or a lie, strife and envy, or wisdom and peace. With astounding ease, we use our tongues but, all too seldom do we consider the damage we do or the potential for absolute good we have. Simplistic though it may seem, the fact of the matter is our tongues are more the servants of our emotions than they are of our convictions. As God's Word verifies, anyone who is in control of his speech is a mature person likened to a horse whose whole body is tamed by the bit in his bridle.

On the other hand, the Bible speaks of the virtual impossibility of controlling our tongues:

> "This is scary. You can tame a tiger, but you can't tame a tongue – it's never been done. The tongue runs wild, a wanton killer. With our tongues we curse the very men and women he made in His image. Curses and blessings out of the same

mouth! My friends, this can't go on" (James 3:7-10, The Message).

This book is in direct response to the statement, "My friends, this can't go on".

We must recognize our inability to control the tongue. At the same moment, we need to realize that God, by His indwelling Spirit, can take the helm within us and give godly direction to what comes out of our mouths!

Once we hear and digest the truth of Solomon's ancient proverb, we see the importance of a book that attempts to detail the tongue's true character and potential.

> "Death and life are in the power of the tongue:
> and they that love it shall eat the fruit thereof"
> (Proverbs 18:21, KJV).

That's awesome!

Charles Fuller

Chapter 1

The Worshipping Tongue

"I cried unto Him with my mouth, and He was extolled with my tongue" (Psalm 66:17, KJV).

It is a skeletal muscle, anchored in our hyoid and jawbone. The surface of it is embedded with four kinds of tiny taste buds. Of all of our body's surface organs it is the one that is the most sensitive to touch. It is that wonderful part of the human anatomy that we call the tongue. It can talk and it can taste. It can become tied and tangled. It can become tacit. It can tattle. It can be truthful. It can be tender. It can be teachable and it can be trouble, spelled with a capital "T". It seems hardly possible that so tiny a body part, when out of control, can be so utterly destructive. Because it is so tiny in comparison to the destruction it can cause, it is not at all unlike an airplane that crashed some years ago. When the investigators finished their survey of the crash scene and analyzed all that had taken place, they came to the conclusion that the accident, that had destroyed not only the plane but also a number of people on board, was caused by the absence of a tiny rivet. It is almost inconceivable that a single missing rivet could cause such a tragedy. Not unlike that, is the awesome destructiveness of the tongue.

When the Lord gave to James the inspiration to write the New Testament letter that bears his name, he inspired him to address a number of very significant issues about this organ called the tongue. The third chapter of James begins like this:

> "Let not many of you become teachers, my brethren, knowing that as such we will incur a stricter judgment" (James 3:1).

Notice the first part of the sentence, "Let not many of you become teachers." That is such good advice. Don't grapple for attention. Don't dash for the spotlight. Don't seek leadership and its recognition for ambition's sake. Because as the Bible states, "To whom much is given, much is required" (Luke 12:48).

It is a somber but accurate reminder that the human spirit is not designed to handle the celebrity we so often seek or give. The daily news stories of scandals and failures among high profile personalities verify the facts... preachers included. We were not made to flirt with pride and get by with it.

> "For we all stumble in many ways. If anyone does not stumble in what he says, he is a perfect man, able to bridle the whole body as well" (James 3:2).

If someone is not offensive with his tongue, he is a mature person; who has not only his tongue under control, but his whole being is spiritually adult.

> "Now if we put the bits into the horses' mouths so that they will obey us, we direct their body as well. Look at the ships also, though they are so great and are driven by strong winds, they are still directed by a very small rudder wherever the inclination of the pilot desires. So also the tongue is a small part of the body, and yet it boasts of

great things. See how great a forest is set aflame by such a small fire" (James 3:3-5)!

It almost takes your breath away when you realize the tremendous power of the tongue. It can do things that are dastardly, destructive, degrading, and distressing. The tongue can lie. It can accuse. It can exaggerate. It can curse. It can deprave. It can slander. It can gossip. I understand a newspaper columnist once said something like this: "Gossip is the fine art of saying nothing in such a way as there is nothing left to be said." It's the match that lights the fire!

Wait just a minute! When the tongue is under control, especially when the tongue is under Christ's control, it is mindboggling what it can do to the contrary. It can encourage. It can tell the truth. It can bless. It can speak love. It can bring hope! And the highest, noblest thing the tongue can do is praise almighty God and proclaim redemption in Jesus Christ. This little organ that has the power to be so destructive when out of control, when under control has the power and the privilege of praising, adoring, exalting, and making known the living God.

There is a passage in the Bible; Psalm 63:3, wherein the psalmist says it so well, "Because your loving kindness is better than life, my lips shall praise You." Let me underscore another passage. In Psalm 51:15-17, where David is dealing with his sin, his confession, his repentance and his restoration unto God, we find this beautiful expression about the use of the tongue:

> "Oh, Lord open my lips that my mouth may declare your praise. For you do not delight in sacrifice, otherwise I would give it; You are not pleased with burnt offering. The sacrifices of God are a broken spirit; A broken and contrite heart Oh God, You will not despise" (Psalm 51:15-17).

In upcoming chapters, we're going to focus our attention on the character of the tongue. We are going to talk about the encouraging tongue. We are going to talk about the acid tongue. We are going to talk about the silent tongue. We are going to talk about the positive tongue. We begin where I suppose we ought to begin; the highest use of the human tongue is namely, to praise and to worship our Lord. Consider four characteristics of a worshipping tongue that brings praise to God's ears and hope to mortal ears.

A worshipping tongue is a <u>pure tongue</u>. Focus your attention again on the 3rd chapter of James, "Now if we put bits into the horses' mouths so that they will obey us we direct their whole body as well" (James 3:3). Just a tiny instrument in the mouth of a horse becomes the way to control and maintain a strong and dynamic animal. Now to verses 8 and 9:

> "But no one can tame the tongue; it is a restless evil and full of deadly poison. With it we bless our Lord and Father, and with it we curse men,

who have been made in the likeness of God" (James 3:8-9).

Amazing isn't it? A tongue, not under the consistent control of the indwelling Spirit, is a tongue that can bless God, on the other hand, I suppose even with the same breath, can curse one made in the similitude of God! James goes on to say,

> "From the same mouth come both blessing and cursing. My brethren, these things ought not to be this way. Does a fountain send out from the same opening both fresh and bitter water" (James 3:10-11)?

Of course not! Neither should there be any thought that a tongue which is impure can be used to bring praise to God. It is not to say that we who have sinned with our tongues can never praise the Lord. It means that it is impossible for a tongue that is in an unrepentant state to be used to bring glory to the Lord. I trust that you and I would not enter a place of worship with any confusion about this. We cannot successfully praise the Lord with a tongue that is engaged in degrading someone else, distorting the truth, or mouthing obscenities. A worshipping tongue is first a pure tongue. The psalmist said:

> "Who may ascend into the hill of the Lord? And who may stand in His holy place? He who has clean hands and a pure heart, who has not

lifted up his soul to falsehood and has not sworn deceitfully" (Psalm 24:3-4).

Who shall approach the Lord? Who shall actually come into the presence of God? One who has clean hands (the symbol of the cleansed life) and a pure heart. The worshipping tongue is one that is confessed, repented, cleansed, and not immediately guilty of being used for some degrading purpose.

Secondly, the worshipping tongue is a <u>prayerful tongue</u>. God in his wisdom and sovereignty has ordained that as we pray, so He functions. I know God is not obligated to me in any way. I know He is not obligated to you in any way. I am fully aware that there is no way we can control the functions, the mind, and the acts of God. God is the independent sovereign judge of all the earth. You do not control God, neither do I. But for some reason, in His gracious economy, He has ordained that when His people pray, He responds. He gives to us the privilege of praying for the sick so that they may be healed. He gives us the privilege of praying for the lost that they may be saved. He gives us the privilege of praying for the nation that it may be preserved. He gives us the joy of praying for each other so that we may be encouraged. He gives us the privilege of making known to Him the hurts and needs of our lives and He responds to those needs as we pray. I cannot tell you why. I do not know anyone who can tell you why. Except in His mercy, generosity, and grace, He has ordained it so. We do not know much about worship, however, until we know something about what it is to use the tongue to address the Holy of Holies; to pray for the church family, to pray for brothers and sisters in Christ, and to pray for the larger family, the Body of Christ. Now do any of us dare walk into the house of God expecting something wonderful to take place, having never asked the Lord for it? Do we pray for the invitation, the moment wherein the gospel is presented and then people are then given the opportunity to respond? Do you exercise the joy of entering into the altar call or invitation period breathing a prayer? "Oh God, give courage, give strength, give conviction, bring someone today to openly respond to Christ; to become part of his Church." Have you learned to do that? A worshipping tongue is not only pure, it is prayerful.

A worshipping tongue is also a <u>peaceful tongue</u>. Opposite is the disruptive tongue; the tongue that is sarcastic, caustic, snide, and hypocritical. It is this type of tongue that divides and destroys the fellowship. It is predictable; it will sour the worshipful atmosphere. A disruptive tongue breaks the spirit of those on whom that tongue is used. A wounded spirit is often unable to worship, unable to experience the exhilaration of the Lord's presence. In the sixth chapter of Proverbs, there is a passage we need to read more often. We do not often think in terms of God's dislike or God's hatred. Interestingly enough, in Proverbs, chapter 6, there is an overt statement about the hatred of God. "There are six things which the Lord hates, Yes seven which are an abomination to Him" (Proverbs 6:16). God hates six things, but the seventh one is even worse than the former six. What are these six things the Lord hates? And what is the seventh that is a pure abomination to him?

1. "haughty eyes"
2. "a lying tongue"
3. "hands that shed innocent blood"
4. "a heart that devises wicked plans"
5. "feet that run rapidly to evil"
6. "a false witness who utters lies"

Have you kept up with your mathematics?

7. "he who spreads strife among brothers"

….It's the match that lights the fire! A worshipping tongue is not a discordant tongue. Do you remember how 1 Corinthians 13 begins, the great love chapter? "If I speak with the tongues of men and of angels but do not have love, I have become a noisy gong or a clanging cymbal." Yes, a worshipping tongue is pure. It is also prayerful. And it is peaceful. And it sows peace among brethren.

A worshipping tongue is a <u>proclaiming tongue</u>. Find time to read the 14th chapter of 1 Corinthians. This is a passage we would not often think of as we talk about worship in general. There we find a focus upon some specific instruction regarding the tongue. Right after the 13th chapter, that is all about love, there comes the trailing 14th chapter and this specific instruction: Paul says,

> "Pursue love, yet desire earnestly spiritual gifts, but especially that you may prophecy" (1 Corinthians 14:10).

Simply put: Pursue love, be zealous for spiritual gifts, but mostly be zealous of the opportunity to communicate the gospel!

> "For one who speaks in a tongue speaks not to men but to God; for no one understands, but in his spirit he speaks mysteries. But one who prophesies speaks to men for edification and exhortation and consolation. One who speaks in a tongue edifies himself; but one who prophesies edifies the church. Now I wish that you all spoke in tongues, but even more that you would prophesy; and greater is one who prophesies than one who speaks in tongues, unless he interprets, so that the church may receive edifying. But now, brethren, if I come to you speaking in tongues what will I profit you unless I speak to you either by way of revelation, or of knowledge, or of prophesy, or of teaching" (1Corinthians 14:2-7)?

Now to pitch a tent on 1Corinthians 14:18-19:

> "I thank God I speak in tongues more than you all; however, in the church I desire to speak five words with my mind so that I may instruct others also, rather than ten thousand words in a tongue."

There are some who believe that the phenomenon of speaking in ecstatic tongues is not for our day. I cannot say that it does not exist today. I have known Christians in whom I have tremendous confidence, who say they do speak in an overflowing prayer language. For the gathered church, I take the wise counsel of Paul, that is, there must be immediate interpretation if it occurs. As he warned, it can be confusing and divisive. He acknowledged his own use of such a tongue but he clearly said, in the church, five words consciously proclaiming the Gospel are to be chosen above 10,000 words in as ecstatic tongue (See 1Corinthians 14:1-9.) There are some who say they experience this phenomenon in private; and I don't think they should restrain themselves. I do point out, however, that the Bible clearly states whether you're speaking in an ecstatic tongue, or a tongue of any description, lest it clearly proclaims and exalts Jesus, it is of little consequence. So when you speak with an ecstatic tongue or with a persuasive tongue or with a formally trained tongue, if you have not clearly presented Jesus Christ, your tongue has been used for little purpose. The worshipping tongue is indeed a proclaiming tongue, making Jesus known. We have to conclude there is no worship, there is no exaltation, and there is no honor to our Lord, until we have proclaimed clearly the Lord Jesus and the way of salvation in Him.

I point back to you that passage we mentioned at the outset. David wrote in the overflow of Psalm 51:

The Awesome Power of the Tongue

"Oh Lord, open thou my lips, and my mouth shall show forth thy praise because you do not desire sacrifice" (Psalm 51:15).

Years ago, I traveled to the Midwest to speak at a retreat for pastors and their wives serving churches in Nebraska and Kansas. On the program was a young woman by the name of Fay. Fay is blind. She is a twin. Her twin sister is sighted. They were prematurely born. They were placed in an incubator. The sister's eyes were not damaged, Fay's were. She said in her late teens and early adult life she was a very bitter, angry person. Then someone led her to the Lord Jesus Christ. He brought about a transformation and placed a sweet spirit within her being. Slowly but surely He gave her a song to match her marvelous voice and talent at the piano. Fay lives in California and she sings in concerts and various meetings throughout the West and Midwest. It was a privilege just to hear her sing. She has a tremendous wit, as do many folk like her, handicapped and blind. For her it's amusing to be in airports, traveling as much as she does. She said, "People can see that I am blind, but the way they deal with it is so interesting. They slow their speech down and simplify it, like, "You…want…to…go…to…the American counter?" She said, "I want to say to them, 'The problem isn't here, (pointing to her ears) it's here' (pointing to her eyes)." There are those who look at her and say, "Can I get you a wheelchair?" "I want to tell them the problem's not my legs. The problem is up here in the eyes. Just let me have your arm, I promise I'll give it back to you."

She sang "Amazing Grace" as part of a mini-concert just before I preached. Her comment was, "If someone had told me fifteen years ago I would be singing before a group of preachers and ministers, 'Amazing Grace how sweet the sound, that saved a wretch like me, I once was blind but now I see'; I would have said, 'Yeah, sure'." As her last number, she sang another simple hymn, but her voice exploded with the message: "This is my story, this is my song; praising my Savior all the day long!" She sang with 20–20 tongue power!

The highest use of that little organ lodged in your mouth and mine is to worship Him. I'm embarrassed over how little I've used it for that purpose; and how much I've used it to degrade, to hurt and to exaggerate. Do you share that embarrassment? I think about how the people of God so quickly and carelessly can verbally dispose of a person. To think, that little instrument, meant to glorify God, I have chosen to use for lesser things. Today without question, the sublimest thing to do with that tongue of yours and mine is to acknowledge openly that Jesus is your Savior and Lord. The King James Version of Psalm 22:3 relates the Lord's presence in the praises of His people. He is at home in the praise of His own. There is a figure of speech used a lot: "That's what I'm talking about!" It's supposed to be an underscoring of how much we agree with what has just been said or done. Worshipping Jesus, praising God, sharing the Gospel, offering hope; <u>that's the tongue I'm talking about!</u>

"Those that hast given so much to me
Give one thing more – a grateful heart;
Not thankful when it pleaseth me,
As if thy blessings had spare days;
But such a heart, whose pulse may be Thy praise."

    From <u>Our Prayer</u>
    George Herbert, 1593–1632
    Masterpieces of Religious Verse,
    (Harper & Brothers, 1948), 118

Chapter 2

The Truthful Tongue

"Therefore, laying aside falsehood, speak truth each one of you with his neighbor, for we are members of one another" (Ephesians 4:25).

The truth was an important commodity around our house when I was growing up. The three worst encounters with discipline I remember as a boy were talking back to my mother, experimenting with a profane word in front of the wrong uncle and the worst one of all, at the grand old age of eight, I told a lie to my dad. He made some impressions upon me that remain to this day. And with each impression he reminded me, "We tell the truth at our house."

My grandfather, Cicero Stuart, was a great back porch philosopher. He taught me a lot of things while he sat about and whittled with his pocket knife. Once he told me, "Son, if you are good at something you won't have to tell people, they'll tell you." I remember he also said, "Son, stay with the facts, choose your words, and take your lumps." Good advice. But, it's awful hard sometimes to stay with the facts and choose your words at the same time. Best you do it, though, because there is a terrible price to pay if you don't. Aldous Huxley, an English writer once was reported as saying something like this: "You shall know the truth and the truth shall make you mad." Of course he was making a play on the words of Jesus. Our Lord said, "You shall know the truth and the truth shall make you free" (John 3:32). The message is, if you know the truth of God, if you know Christ Himself, who is The Truth; then, indeed, you are free. You are free from the bondage of sin and its consequences. You're free of all the encumbrances of unbelief. You are free of the need to distort and exaggerate; free of hiding the truth or hiding from it.

When a person knows the truth, but can't seem to tell the truth, that person is in bondage of another kind. It is vital not only for Christians to know the truth, believe the truth, preach the truth, teach the truth, and sing the truth; but also it is just as vital that we tell the truth. Otherwise there is a high price to pay.

> "So this I say, and affirm together with the Lord, that you walk no longer just as the Gentiles walk, in the futility of their mind, being darkened in their understanding, excluded from the life of God because of the ignorance that is in them, because of the hardness (blindness, KJV) of their heart; and they having become callous, have given themselves over to sensuality for the practice of every kind of impurity with greediness. But you did not learn Christ in this way, if you have heard Him and have been taught in Him, just as the truth is in Jesus, that in reference to your former manner of life, you lay aside the old self, which is being corrupted in accordance with the lusts of deceit and that you be renewed in the spirit of your mind, and put on the new self which in the likeness of God has been created in righteousness and holiness of the truth. Therefore laying aside falsehood speak truth each one of you with his neighbor, for we are members of one another" (Ephesians 4:17-25).

Paul says in verse 17, "walk not (live not) like other Gentiles walk (live)". When referring to Gentiles, Paul is speaking of unbelievers. He goes on to identify the heathen as those who cannot understand the lifestyle of the Christian because of the "hardness" of their hearts.

When Paul speaks of an unbeliever's blindness he refers to more than the inability to see, but to a "hardness" that obstructs understanding. The Greek word for hardness is, "porosis", denoting a rigidity that will not allow spiritual perception. It is a graphic way to describe an impervious mind or unteachable heart.

A heart that remains disinterested and disobedient to God eventually comes to what Paul describes in verse 19 as, "having become callous" (past feeling, KJV) and without conscience. Some diabetics can quickly identify with the meaning of "past feeling". Though there can be feeling in the feet and lower extremities of a diabetic, the feeling is that to the hand, a shoe or some general touch. However, a sharp pointed touch or a solid blow simply cannot be felt. In other words, some things for certain diabetics are beyond feeling. It is disturbing to realize people can be reached by many appeals to the mind but to the specific truth of God, they are past feeling!

> "And they having become callous have given themselves over to sensuality for the practice of every kind of impurity with greediness. But you did not learn Christ in this way, if indeed you have heard him and have been taught in Him, just as truth is in Jesus" (Ephesians 4:19-21).

The fact of the matter is there may be some of you who claim that you have come to know Christ, but it may be that you have not, says Paul. But if you have heard Christ and if you have been taught by Christ, then this is not what you have been taught to do. He goes on to tell the Ephesians to put off concerning the former conversation, or lifestyle, the old man. The old man is the one untouched by redemption; what you used to be when you were not a Christian, and that is corrupt according to the deceitful lusts. Rather we are to be renewed in the spirit of our mind and put on the new man. That new man is the twice born man, the one that is the new person in Christ that God has created in righteousness and true holiness. Now comes the bottom line:

> "Therefore, laying aside falsehood speak truth each one of you with his neighbor; for we are members of one another" (Ephesians 4:25).

Before we take another step we need to take note that there are at least three definite results among God's people for not telling the truth. I may claim to know the truth, to know Christ. Furthermore, I not only know the truth I may preach the truth. My orthodoxy may be a foregone conclusion. But if I can't tell the truth, I have another problem. There are definite consequences for untruthfulness that are obvious here. First, if you are one who claims to know the truth but can't tell the truth, you actually encourage people to be cynical about what it means to be a Christian. There is enough cynicism as is. There is enough skepticism about the Faith in our world as is; we need not contribute more to it. But if you are not an honest person, though you claim to know Christ, then what you do is just simply encourage people to be cynical about the whole proposition of what it is to be a child of God.

In the second place, if you are not a truthful Christian then you entertain Satan as a welcome guest. Look at Paul's advice in Ephesians 4:27, "And do not give the devil an opportunity." It is all part of the same context. The word "place" means occasion or opportunity. It can mean "encouragement". Read the passage that way: "Neither give encouragement to the devil." He doesn't need much. Why would you want to encourage him; or welcome him into your life? Why give him a place where he can settle in upon your life? You do, in fact, encourage him if you are basically a dishonest person.

The third result of Christians not being truthful with one another is that we endanger the health of the Lord's church. Focus on all of Ephesians 4:25, "Therefore, laying aside falsehood, speak truth each one of you with his neighbor, for we are members of one another." As Christians we're part of the same body, that is, the body of Christ. One part of the body must be honest with another part of the body or the whole body suffers. For instance, my hands have in them the capacity of sense or touch. Let's say I put my hand close to a hot stove, but my brain lies to my hand and does not send the signal, "That's hot!" Instead my hand comes close to that hot unit and says, "That's not hot, that won't hurt you." The brain sends back the repeated lie, "That won't hurt, put your hand on it." Somebody is about to get hurt! Obviously one part of the body can't lie to another part of the body without endangering the whole body. That's the point. You endanger the health of the body of Christ if you are a dishonest part of it.

Now with that observation made I want to spend some important moments talking about the 6 basic characteristics of the truthful tongue.

1. First of all, a truthful tongue is a <u>credible tongue</u>. That is, it has integrity. I cannot think of a time in modern day evangelical Christianity where the subject of credibility is any more important than it is today. There are people who are bewildered. There are people who are disillusioned. There are people who are angry. There are people in all quarters of life today who are disturbed because those of high profile have been found to lack integrity. They're not credible.

   There are three keys to credibility. The first one is accuracy. Exaggeration sometimes is little more than a denial of the truth, or the distortion of the truth. Sometimes we get cute and say, "God understands, it's just a little white lie." I'm not too sure that God ever colors lies white, black, grey, or anything else. If it's inaccurate, and we know it is, it's dishonest. Make a note: a white lie will damn somebody just as quickly as a black one. Inaccuracy can be the match that starts the fire! Secondly, I think the word attitude applies to a credible tongue. So many times I want the truth to prevail, but the reason I want the truth to prevail is that I want to be vindicated. I want the truth to serve my posture, my position. What we should want is an attitude that vindicates our Lord. We want the truth to verify and vindicate the truth, not our version of the truth. If we have an attitude that is smug and judgmental, seeking to defeat and embarrass others, then our motives are untruthful! The third word I would use to describe the keys to credibility is the word action. Do we demand more truth from others than we demand of ourselves? That's where push comes to shove, doesn't it? If we have not consciously committed ourselves to be truthful then our expectation of truth from others becomes a self-awarded, self-righteous license for witch-hunting.

2. A second quality of the truthful tongue is that of a <u>considerate tongue</u>. It is not only credible, it is considerate. To be even more thorough, there are three keys to a considerate tongue. First is commendation. A considerate tongue seeks to be a commending tongue. It looks for the best. There are times wherein the critical tongue must be used but, criticism that is not couched in courtesy and balanced with commendation usually will come across as being not at all constructive. The second key is criticism. Proverbs 7:6 says it, and says it well, "Faithful are the wounds of a friend." If you love someone, if you genuinely want him to be his best, you very well may have to offer criticism. Sometimes we hear someone described

as being "brutally frank." Often, such persons are really more brutal than they are frank. If you are basically given to commendation and to courtesy, then your frankness will not become brutality. That leads to the third key to a considerate tongue; courtesy. Common courtesy gives the benefit of the doubt. Common courtesy chooses times for confrontation. Common courtesy does not dominate a conversation. Common courtesy allows for human worth.

3. The third quality of a truthful tongue is a <u>confessional tongue</u>. There are some very honest statements every Christian must learn to use if he or she is going to be truthful. The first such statement is "I was wrong, I was wrong". Do you remember the television series called "Happy Days"? If so, you remember The Fonz. Fonzerelli never could admit he was wrong. He simply could not use those words. Occasionally he would be absolutely indefensible; he was wrong. He would try to say it, "I was wrrr, I was wrrr…" He couldn't form the words! Finally he would say, "I was mistaken." You can't be honest if you cannot acknowledge that you can be wrong. Secondly, you must be able to say, "I don't know." Now, that's very difficult for some of us but what is so terribly wrong with not knowing something? You cannot be teachable until you admit the need to learn. Besides, who wants to be thought of as a proverbial "know it all"? The third confessing essential to a truthful tongue is, "I am a Christian." If peer pressure and circumstance can

so press you that you cannot bring yourself to openly acknowledge you are a Christian; you have a problem. As a Christian, you will not be totally honest. How can we be truthful if we withhold or deny the most important truth about who we are? We must be comfortable with three statements if we are to be truthful: I was wrong. I don't know. I am a Christian.

4. The truthful tongue is a <u>consistent tongue</u>. We sometimes say with a kind of a wry smile and with tongue in cheek, "Do as I say not as I do." That's a terrible role to follow. Some years ago I received a letter from the local Academy of Medicine, and I am sure that local pastors of all denominations received that letter. The local Academy of Medicine is made up, I think, of about 400 members. The Academy stated their concern about cigarette smoking; realizing most people begin the habit before they are eighteen years of age. Therefore they underscored the importance of good adult role models who can say, "Do as I do". The medical academy's letter encouraged local churches to establish a policy prohibiting smoking anywhere in their facilities. "If you do not have a policy in your church where you do not permit smoking consider a no smoking policy in your church." Furthermore the letter went on to say, "Please call upon adults not to violate the policy you establish." I understand why this physician's group is saying that and I commend them for taking the initiative, but isn't

it sad that you have to admonish adult church members, "Do as I say, and say as I do." The Academy was simply stating the truth of the matter; we have little to say unless we are consistent with what we say. And that pertains to things other than just smoking; it pertains to the whole issue of our influence.

5. A truthful tongue is a <u>crusader's tongue</u>. At times, it needs to become outspoken. Your convictions, the circumstances that surround you, obvious injustices, and pernicious evils almost demand that you assume some kind of openness and assertiveness; and that you embrace some kind of a cause. Sometimes you need to become a crusader.

Now, any Christian has to ask himself five simple questions, before becoming involved in something that is a crusade or a cause:

-Is this a substitute for personal evangelism?

-Is it something that makes me rob time and allegiance from my own church?

-Is it contrary to Christian values and behavior?

-Is it something that inflates your ego and makes your opponent inferior to you?

-Is it constructive in nature, or destructive in its character?

6. The final quality of a truthful tongue is that it's a <u>compelling tongue</u>. It is the kind of tongue that causes people to want to listen to the rest of what you have to say.

It is the kind of tongue that gives veracity to all else that is spoken. It is the kind of tongue that is a notarization of the whole of your witness. Two statements are worth their weight in gold when spoken of Christians: "If he said it, you can go to the bank with it." And another compelling remark: "You can live and die by what that person tells you!" What tremendous commendations for a compelling tongue.

In the first few verses of 2 Corinthians 4, the Apostle Paul refers to his own ministry. This letter to the believers in Corinth is less corrective than Paul's first. 2 Corinthians is a bit more gentle, certainly more personable. As Paul talks about his own ministry, he says some things that are very important for us to hear again. Beginning at the very first of the chapter:

> "Therefore since we have this ministry, as we received mercy, we do not lose heart. But we have renounced the things hidden because of shame, not walking in craftiness or adulterating the word of God, but by the manifestation of truth; commending ourselves to every man's conscience in the sight of God. And even if our gospel is veiled, it is veiled to those who are perishing in whose case the god of this world has blinded the minds of the unbelieving so that they might not see the light of the gospel of the glory of Christ, who is the image of God" (2 Corinthians 4:1-4).

Paul obviously means, if the gospel does not come across clearly, it is not hidden because we have hidden it. It is not hidden because we've obscured it. It is not hidden because we have dealt with it deceitfully. It is not hidden because we have failed to give it verification and veracity. It is hidden because the god of this world has blinded their minds. It is so crucial, that people hear, understand, and believe the gospel because we have not obscured it, neither have made it unbelievable. If the lost stay lost it should not be because we have presented to them a thwarted, contorted gospel; that is somehow blighted by our dishonesty. It is simply because they refuse and succumb to the darkness that the prince of this world has given to them. Read on:

> "For we do not preach ourselves but Christ Jesus as Lord, and ourselves as your bond-servants for Jesus' sake. For God, who said, "light shall shine out of darkness" is the one who has shone in our hearts to give the light of the knowledge of the glory of God in the face of Christ. But we have this treasure in earthen vessels. So that the surpassing greatness of the power will be of God and not from ourselves" (2 Corinthians 4:5-7).

The excellency of the treasure of Christ is Christ Himself, the Truth. We have God, the Holy Spirit, dwelling in us. We have this treasure, the gospel of Christ Himself, in earthen vessels. That rendition, "earthen vessels" refers to a common clay pot.

We have in our very being the Spirit of Christ; hence, we have the treasure of Gospel truth imbedded within us! We have Christ Himself dwelling in this physical body. Strange, isn't it? It defies any explanation. Why would God want to take up residence in a common clay vessel and reside there? The answer rebounds; so that the likeness of Jesus may be seen in us but He may be the one who is honored!

I am looking at a small clay jar on my desk. It is nothing more than hardened red mud. If I drop it, it will crack. It's just a clay jar, nothing else. There is something inside of it, however, that is a real treasure. It is my mother's engagement ring. It was given to her by my dad in 1925. He was a young railroad man who probably worked his head off to be able to buy that ring and give it to his bride. I treasure it along with several other things that were hers. You would agree that a clay jar is no place to be keeping a treasure like that. Just doesn't seem a likely place for it. That's the point. The point is that if anything of God is to be seen in us, it's not to be because of the vessel. It's because of Him, who dwells in the vessel. The excellency is not of the vessel, but it is the treasure in the vessel. On the other hand, a botched, cracked, ugly vessel can be so distracting the treasure in it is never considered. That's why it's important that Christians tell and live the truth. It's not enough to say, "I know the truth! I preach the truth! I sing the truth!" It's important that we uphold the Truth by living it and telling it. The ultimate witness for the Christian is that Jesus Christ is the Truth and where He is, the truth is spoken!

Dr. Charles Fuller

"The greatest friend of truth is time,
her greatest enemy is prejudice
And her constant companion is humility."

Charles Caleb Colton
Instant Quotation Dictionary,
(Career Institute, Inc., 1969), 259

Chapter 3

The Forgiving Tongue

"Jesus said unto him, I say not unto you, until seven times: but until seventy times seven…" (Matthew 18:22, KJV).

One of Paul's admonitions to the Christians in Ephesus is delightfully picturesque. When he comes to what we call the 5th chapter of that letter, he begins it like this, "Therefore be imitators of God as beloved children and walk in love as Christ also has loved us" (v. 1-2). The word that is translated "imitators" is the Greek word from whence we get our words mimic, imitation, or imitator. So if you really translate what he says in language we would use today, he said, "Therefore be imitators of God like dear children are mimics of their parents and walk in love as Christ also loved you." We all know that children learn much of what they learn by imitation. They mimic their parents. They mimic the adult world around them. Sometimes they mimic their peers. But by and large they grow and become who they are by mimicking the adults around them.

Christians, children of God, can learn to become Christ-like by imitating our Lord. The problem is that if we just imitate or mimic our Lord in terms of words or appropriate behavior, we very well may find ourselves able to use the right words, carry off the right demeanor, but be void of the right spirit to generate that behavior when the pressure is on. Many of us know how to give devotionals, for instance, on the subject of forgiveness. We know the right words to say. We know the right passages to emphasize. We even know how to make people feel guilty because they are not forgiving. We sit around taking copious notes on sermons and lessons about forgiveness. But our problem is not that we don't know how to mimic the words, we even know how to use the words at the right time.

But when the pressure is on… when we are under the gun… when somebody offends us, then are we able to use the right words? So often our problem is we know the right words if the conditions are appropriate, but when we are under fire… when somebody offends us… when it is our character that is up for grabs, momentarily we explode and revert back to the old vocabulary. The result? There is not a bit of difference between us and someone who has never known the Lord. So it's not a matter of just mimicking godly vocabulary. It's not a matter of stretching our behavior across the example of Christ when the moments are conducive. It's a matter of capturing the spirit of Christ that lies behind the words.

Take the time to look into John 13. Now, let's focus our attention on the Lord. Let's watch Him as He forgives and ask the question in the process; "Is our Lord worth imitating?" If the conditions are right, if the circumstances are conducive, He is able to be forgiving. What is the response when someone tries to get under His skin? What is the reaction when His forgiveness quotient is put to the test? That is what is well worth watching.

"Jesus became troubled in spirit, and testified and He said, Truly, Truly…" (v. 21). Those two words, truly, truly, appear often in Scripture. It is a Biblical way to say: I'm telling you the truth. I'm not lying to you. I want you to hear me. It's a double emphasis. "Truly, truly, I say to you, that one of you will betray me." Why did Jesus, in that upper room, say this to those gathered disciples? Why did He announce, before the fact, "One of you is going to betray me"? I really don't know; except I wonder if it could be that Jesus was saying, "<u>Before</u> this happened I chose the man, I knew what I was doing." You see, it could be, after all of this was over, the disciples might be talking and one of them could say, "You know, Judas had been traveling with us for three years and he betrayed our Lord. Why didn't Jesus know that all along? He was supposed to know everything. Why didn't He know that?" They could conclude Jesus had a faulty omniscience. But Jesus made it very plain. "I know what I'm doing. I knew it then, I know it now; one of you is going to betray me."

> "The disciples began looking at one another, at a loss to know of which one He was speaking. There was reclining on Jesus' bosom one of His disciples whom Jesus loved. (That's John.) So Simon Peter gestured to him, (that is to John), and said to him, 'Tell us who it is of whom He is speaking'" (John 13:22-24).

Can't you get the picture? Just let yourself into that upper room for a moment. Here sits John next to Jesus, on His right. Peter is down the way and gets John's attention and whispers, "John, ask Him who it is." Find out. Get the word." John, leaning back on Jesus bosom, said to Him, "Lord who is it?"

In Matthew 26:22-25, you'll find the parallel to this same incident. Matthew says that when this moment came every one of them, around the table began to say, "Is it I? Is it I? Is it I?" Now you've got to give it to them. You have to commend that spirit. Isn't it interesting they did not say, "I know who it is!"

Can't you imagine Simon Peter thinking to himself, "I know who it is! I've got that figured out. It's Thomas! You can't trust him, he doubts everybody." Or can't you hear Thomas whispering to himself, "I know who it is! It's Peter! Peter's always sounding off, can't live up to what he says." Rather, every one of them said, "Is it I?" Not too long before all this, when Jesus said that He was going to the cross, Peter resisted, "Lord, not you!" Jesus said, "Get behind me, Satan" (Matthew 16:22–23). You recall it was then that Peter insisted, "Even though all may fall away because of You, I will never fall away." Jesus said to him, "Truly I say to you that this very night, before a rooster crows, you will deny Me three times" (Matthew 26:33-34). You have to wonder if Simon Peter was thinking about that when the Lord said, one of you is going to betray me. Peter suddenly was not so sure of himself, and he said, "Is it I?"

There is something we need to realize along with these disciples. In this upper-room moment they recognized that every last one of them was capable of betraying Him. And I remind you; we too, are capable of doing whatever a mortal can do. Taking offense, you may say, "Not I! My backbone won't collapse that easily!" I beg your pardon. You are capable of doing whatever a mortal can do, and so am I. So, is it I? Is it you!?

> "Jesus answered, 'This is the one for whom I shall dip the morsel and give it to him.' So when He had dipped the morsel, He took and gave it to Judas, the son of Simon Iscariot. After the morsel, Satan then entered into him. Therefore

Jesus said to him, 'What you do, do quickly.' Now no one of those reclining at the table knew for what purpose He had said this to him. For some were supposing, because Judas had the money box, that Jesus was saying to him, buy the things we have need of for the feast or else, that He should give something to the poor" (Matthew 13:26-29).

They didn't know exactly what Jesus meant by what He said. Let me remind you of the setting. In that day they did not sit at tables. They reclined. Men either reclined around a rug on which food was served or at a low table. Women served the table but generally they did not eat at the table. As the men reclined, they propped themselves on the left side and they sopped with the right hand. We know John was on Jesus' right; therefore his head would have rested on Jesus' chest. Now, who was on Jesus' left? Apparently it was Judas. Traditionally, the host placed on his right and on his left two people he particularly wanted to recognize. Often they were the places of honor. Interestingly enough, if Judas was on His left, Jesus' head rested on Judas' chest. Now there was a moment in formal dinners where the host would take a piece of bread or meat and would sop it into a dish. And he would give the sop to someone he wanted to honor; usually the person on the left or the right. Jesus sopped and he handed the morsel to Judas. What did he mean by doing that? It could be it was a non-verbal plea, "Judas, don't do it! Don't do it, man!" Was that what he meant? Having been given the morsel Judas left immediately and finished the process of betraying Jesus. In short order came Gethsemane, Jesus' arrest, His crucifixion, and praise God, His resurrection!

To this point what we've seen is the display of Jesus' mercy, His forgiveness, kindness, and generosity. But let's take Him out of the upper room; after all, the upper room had a certain degree of security to it. The only people there were Jesus and His disciples. Let's take Jesus out of the Passover setting and put Him out on the firing line. Let's put Him out there where He's the object of abuse and let's see how His forgiveness quotient registers. After all, what good is it to imitate somebody when the conditions are conducive? Let's put Him under different conditions; and see if He's worth imitating. Let's go from the upper room, across Kidron, up the hill to Gethsemane; their retreat site, to the garden of prayer. Let's watch Jesus in Gethsemane as He knelt and prayed. Sweat, like great drops of blood, fell to the ground as he bore the weight of the sin of the world upon Him. His disciples, whom He had asked to watch and pray with Him for an hour, fell asleep. Now Jesus comes out from that prayerful experience with an enormous burden upon Him; bearing the sin of the world for which He's going to die. And then Judas arrives with the arresting soldiers carrying torches and weapons. By prior agreement Judas is going to kiss the face of the one they are to arrest. After all, it is dark. He is going to kiss the one they're to arrest so there will be no mistaken identity. As Judas comes with his arresting entourage, and approaches Jesus, let's discover what Jesus' forgiveness quotient is like. Can He handle it? What does He say to Judas as he approaches Him? Of all things the Scripture tells us He said, "Hail, friend." Hail, <u>friend</u>? What was He saying? Could it be again, even as when He dipped the sop, He was saying, "Man, don't do it. Don't do it." As Judas, the Betrayer, stood there, Jesus gave him every reason to know he could be forgiven and start over!

Some years ago I was in California to speak for a seminary graduation. I was deeply impressed by a young man whom I saw come across the commencement platform twice. He received two master's degrees; one in Theology and one in Religious Education. I didn't know he was going to get the two degrees though I met him the evening before at the student reception. I was impressed with him then, simply by hearing his story. He was a young man who had been quite a renegade, raised in a very conservative Christian home. He became involved in a number of the counter cultures; among them the drug culture, San Francisco variety. He eventually became destitute. When he was in that state he came across some Christians who displayed love, grace, and patience toward him and led him to an encounter with Jesus. He was saved. After his conversion he sensed that God was calling him into the ministry. He enrolled in seminary and in a period of four years had done the work to earn two seminary degrees. As he marched across the platform and received those two degrees, I could not help but think what a horrible, mistake it would have been had those Christians who met this young man had only seen the drug-daze in his eyes, the long stringy hair and his surly mouth. What if they had only seen a disheveled rebel and concluded, "Forget it, no hope! Forget it, he can't be reached." What a tragedy! Thank God for somebody who understood something about the grace of Jesus. Now the world has a trained, zealous preacher on its hands!

Learn something indispensable from Jesus in Gethsemane, <u>the lesson of patience</u>. It is to learn there is no real forgiveness until there is patience.

Now we leave Gethsemane and go to Golgotha. On a hill called Golgotha, Jesus is going to be under fire. Let's find out what kind of forgiveness quotient He has there. Luke tells us in the 23rd chapter of his gospel that Jesus on the cross said, "Father, forgive them, for they do not know what they are doing" (v. 34). Now, what exactly does that mean? Just take the time to look at the entire account. You will find He was abused and tested at several points. He sustained <u>injury</u>. Luke tells us the Roman soldiers crucified Him. Before they crucified Him, they spat upon Him, they beat Him, and put a crown of thorns on his head. He was severely abused. Then he was nailed to a Roman instrument of execution, a cross. In those moments of physical abuse and injury, what did He cry? "Father, forgive them." Jesus forgave His tormentors for they had no idea whom they were subjecting to this painful injury.

Jesus suffered <u>insinuation</u>. The scribes and elders at the cross said, "He saved others; He cannot save Himself. He is the King of Israel; let Him now come down from the cross, and we will believe in Him. He trusts in God; let God rescue Him now, if He delights in Him, for He said, 'I am the Son of God'" (Matthew 27:42-43). They insinuated He was not what He said He was. I don't know about you, but I doubt that I could handle that much demeaning insinuation. Imagine being labeled a fraud; a complete fake. That's tough, that's hard to take. Yet resounding from the cross came Jesus' words, "Father, forgive them."

What else was a test to Jesus' forgiveness? There was <u>insult</u>. In the language of the Hebrew, the Roman, and the Greek, a sign was placed above his head, "This is King of the Jews." It was not meant to be a compliment. It was a brazen insult. Unknown to the executioners, He <u>was</u> the King of Kings. Injured, insinuated against, insulted, He said, "Father, forgive them." When you speak about imitating Jesus you're not talking about just saying the right words. You're talking about having a supernatural spirit that lies behind those words.

Travel up to Galilee after Jesus was raised from the dead. In fact, the angel said to the women at the empty tomb, "But go, tell His disciples and Peter, 'He is going ahead of you to Galilee; there you will see Him, just as He told you" (Mark 16:7). The reason for the second part of that instruction is obvious. Of all the disciples, Peter had let Him down the most. All of them had fled from Gethsemane, every last one of them. But Peter was the one who had made such sweeping statements about his loyalty and that he would not fold under pressure, that of course, he did. A lasting picture we have of Simon Peter is that of him weeping copiously. He was broken because he realized he had done the very thing he said he would never do. So there was significance in the message Jesus sent ahead to the disciples. He said He would meet them in Galilee but He especially wanted to see Peter. They did meet there and we know He and Peter had a private talk. After a big catch of fish, they had a fish fry breakfast. But while the other disciples were bringing the catch to the beach, Jesus and

Simon Peter talked alone; because Simon swam to the seashore by himself. We also know the two of them talked after breakfast as well. Little doubt, they talked about Peter's denial. Surely, Peter was full of regret and repentance, knowing he deserved an, "I told you so". Peter's apology was to be expected, but Jesus wanted him to learn a lesson in grace. I would imagine Jesus said something like, "Simon, do you remember the day when I was trying to teach you something about forgiveness? You asked if it is enough to forgive somebody seven times. And I answered, seventy times seven." Perhaps He went on to say, "Simon, do you remember the day I first met you, and said, 'You are Simon the son of John, but you're going to be Peter, a rock?' Peter, I'm here to tell you that I knew what I was saying when I made that statement. I'm here to persist. I'm going to give you the strength to be what you don't have in yourself." And Simon Peter was on his way to becoming The Rock.

In Gethsemane, Jesus displayed the quality of <u>patience</u>. On Golgotha there is seen the quality of <u>humility</u>. Along the Sea of Galilee He offered the quality of <u>compassion</u>.

Forgiveness, after the fashion of Jesus, awaits our willingness to be overtaken by a spirit of patience, humility, and compassion. Such forgiveness has everything to do with our capacity to be children of God. What does the Word of God say? It states, "Therefore be imitators of God, as beloved children" (Ephesians 5:1).

John's 13:30 makes for an interesting study: "So after receiving the morsel he went out immediately, and it was night." Consider that last phrase, "And it was night." Judas had received the gesture of forgiveness, turned a deaf ear to it and he walked out into the night. It was not just physical night. It was a convicting night! It was dark. It was foreboding. It was bleak. It is night for anybody who is offered the sop of forgiveness from Jesus; and he turns a deaf ear to it. And for you and me to accept the sop, that is the forgiveness of Christ, and then refuse to extend that forgiveness to somebody else, it's night! It's dark! It's ugly! If you have accepted Christ's forgiveness, now comes the penetrating question. Are you willing to pass it on?

So there we have it. From Jesus' version of forgiveness we learn there is a trinity of unmistakable components: patience, humility, and compassion. A tongue that learns words of patience, of humility, and compassion; is a tongue that can speak the language of forgiveness!

"When we have sinned against another, we should go and ask for his or her forgiveness….this is walking out abandonment to Jesus. Our pride will fiercely fight it."

Jerald R. White, Jr.,
The Spirit and Presence of Christ, (Xulon Press, 2005), 86

Chapter 4

The Imploring Tongue

"And at the evening sacrifice I arose up from my heaviness and having rent my garment and my mantle, I fell on my knees and spread out my hands unto the Lord my God" (Ezra 9:5, KJV).

Prayer is conversation with God. There are times when the conversation is warm; overflowing with praise and gratitude. There are times when that conversation is intense and burdened. There are times wherein the conversation is brief. There are times when it is exhaustive. But, mark it down, prayer, our conversation with God, is absolutely essential. It is essential to the wholesomeness and health of a Christian's life.

Prayer is indispensable to our <u>relationship</u> with God. It is quite obvious that we cannot have much of a relationship with God while not on speaking terms with Him. As with anyone, you cannot have a vital relationship and at the same time not communicate with that person. For instance, it is difficult for children to gain the impression there is a vital, wholesome relationship between their parents and God if the only conversation with God they hear is the occasional expression of thanks at a meal. Relationship is the first area wherein conversation with God is absolutely indispensable.

Our communication with God is equally linked to <u>stewardship</u>. God has endowed us, and imbued us, with certain gifts and abilities. He's given us a calling. As His Church we have a commission as a body of believers to evangelize the world. How could it be possible that we would be able to pursue the mind of God concerning our gifts, concerning His design upon our lives, and concerning our commission to evangelize a world, and never communicate with Him?

Not only in terms of our relationship and our stewardship, but also in terms of the <u>fellowship</u> of God's people, our conversations with God are absolutely indispensable. One of the great studies in the Bible, reflecting the impact of prayer, or the lack of it, when God's people pray or don't, is found in Matthew's account of Gethsemane. There, with a burden of sin's guilt upon Him, sweating, as it were great drops of blood, upon the ground; Jesus asked His disciples to watch with Him for one hour. The word, "watch" does not mean simply to look or to peer. It means, literally, to stay awake. Jesus said I must go yonder and pray. And he went the distance of a stone's throw. He was asking His disciples to share this fellowship of prayer and anguish for one hour. Three times He emerged from prayer to find them asleep. You remember the disappointment Jesus expressed: "So, you men could not keep watch with Me for one hour" (Matthew 26:40)? Of course I cannot be too critical of those disciples because I'm embarrassed about how many times I've fallen asleep on the Lord. But note the change among those same disciples in just a matter of a few days. After the Resurrection and Ascension, and following the instruction of the Lord they spent ten days in confession, in repentance, sharing, praying, and waiting. Suddenly the Holy Spirit came upon them like no group of believers has ever been visited. The difference in those disciples afterward was the difference between the power of prayer and the absence of it!

Another area of life wherein conversation with God is absolutely indispensable obviously is in <u>worship</u>. How can we worship the Lord and not have an exchange of communication with Him whereby He speaks to us in and through the Scriptures? How can the Holy Spirit manifest His presence and power and there be no communication between His Spirit and our spirit? In any honest thought about prayer and worship, especially prayer and <u>public</u> worship, there is a loaded question to be answered: When we pray, to whom are we speaking? We need to think. We need to concentrate. To whom are we speaking when we pray? I've heard well meaning, but unthinking people, even ministers who should know better, as they have used prayer essentially as a time to make announcements or perhaps they use prayer as a means to hand out subtle compliments, or to inform God about things that God already knows. Prayer has been used to fill time gaps while distractions are addressed or mechanical corrections are made. Come now, to whom are we talking when we pray? Are we talking to each other? We've all heard prayers with rambling, disjointed sentences made up of words, but no real conversation with the God of the universe was taking place. Be reminded, when we <u>do</u> pray, we are talking to our Eternal Father, the Sovereign Judge of all the earth! That is considerably more significant than an audience with the Pope, an introduction to an NFL star, or a conversation with the President of the United States!

Please concentrate with me on what I believe are some very definite characteristics of genuine prayer. Remember, we are talking about the tongue. With this chapter we address the language spoken by the imploring tongue. And why would I identify the praying tongue as the "imploring tongue"? The word "imploring" seems to add dimensions of depth and passion to a spiritual function that is all too often a perfunctory one. We use the word so seldom these days; we probably need the dictionary to define it. Looking into one of the dictionaries on my desk, I find the word imploring defined in terms like: to beseech, to entreat, to cry out, and to pray earnestly. I chose to caption this chapter, the Imploring Tongue, because prayer may be relaxed but it is not indifferent. It should be normal to a Christian's life but not ordinary. A praying tongue is earnest and imploring or it misses its purpose. The imploring tongue is a <u>reverent tongue</u>. We've just finished considering that very emphasis, have we not? It is a reverent tongue. Remember what we've already said; Think, think, concentrate on who it is you are talking to when you pray. It makes all the difference in the world in terms of reverence. Put the matter into perspective: When praying, you are talking with the Creator of the Universe, who has not only made Himself approachable; He has assumed the role of our Heavenly Father. And why? Because we matter to Him! It's not a situation that prompts pride in us, but gratitude and reverence.

Focus with me on three direct, simple verses where our Lord gives us instruction about the reverence of prayer; Matthew 6:5-7:

> "When you pray, you are not to be like the hypocrites; for they love to stand and pray in the synagogues and on the street corners so that they may be seen by men. Truly, I say to you, they have their reward in full."

To whom are they speaking? They are speaking to their peers. To whom are they talking? They're talking to anyone who will listen. They have their reward.

"But you, when you pray, go into your inner room, close the door and pray to your Father who is in secret and your Father who sees what is done in secret will reward you. And when you are praying, do not use meaningless repetition as the Gentiles do, for they suppose that they will be heard for their many words."

There are, even today, religions that emphasize repetition; even to the point of being mesmerized, thinking that repetition is that which brings about success in meditation. It's not new. What is Jesus saying here? Is He suggesting there is no place for public prayer among God's people? Certainly not. Jesus prayed publicly. He prayed openly. There was that day He prayed and His disciples, having heard Him pray said, "Lord, teach us to pray" (Luke 11:1). It was not that they had never prayed. These were Jewish men who prayed often and dutifully. That was a part of their lives. But they had never heard someone pray the way Jesus prayed. And they said, having heard Him, "Lord, (Master, Rabbi,) teach us to pray." No, this is not instruction to never pray publicly. This is instruction to concentrate on the One to whom you speak. Do not pray for others to hear and approve. It is to be like entering into a private place, closing the door and having a conversation with God, the Father, as if He were the only one with you. The instruction then is two-fold. Simply this, first: <u>Do not pray to impress those about you</u>, remember to whom you speak. Secondly: <u>Do not insist that other people pray to your satisfaction</u>. Some of us as Christians are critical about how others pray. We may be listening for favorite prayer words or doctrinal expressions that constitute "real" prayer. Don't insist that others pray to your satisfaction, nor pray so that others might be impressed with your prayer.

The prayerful tongue is a reverent tongue because we know the One to whom we speak. I believe that the Scriptures also teach us that a prayerful tongue is a <u>ready</u> tongue. When Paul was writing his first letter to the Christians in Thessalonica, he gave them a sequence of admonitions. One of them was pray without ceasing (1 Thessalonians 5:17). Just what does that mean? Does that suggest that we are to go about mumbling, as it were, constantly repeating phrases of prayer? Of course not, it means three very definite things. Obviously it means that we're to live in the frame of mind whereby we always can pray. Stretching Paul's instruction beyond the Thessalonians to us, we could interpret the verse to mean, "Keep your heart and mind clean and clear enough so you could pray at the drop of a hat." It also means to live with prayer as a way to deal with everyday life. Prayer is not just an escapist fashion of dealing with the unwanted and unpleasant. Prayer is a legitimate, <u>realistic</u> way in which to deal with life, come what may. Simply put, the way of prayer is the way to live.

Years ago I met a woman, a Christian, who has been diagnosed as a manic depressive. For nineteen years she suffered from that emotional disorder. It was estimated that she spent about 60% of her time in the depressive side of that up and down mentality. She shared with me that she, along with her doctors, and friends, and counselors, struggled with how one lives with this condition as a Christian. She said she came to realize that she could not live with it on the basis of circumstances. It is circumstance that often brings about radical mood change. She said she learned that you cannot live with this situation victoriously by attempting to feign happiness. She learned there is one way to live with this manic depressive problem, and that is to live in a vital daily walk with Christ. Her testimony was, "I've discovered that I can live joyously as a Christian even though this malady is with me constantly; if I maintain a daily, constant, <u>realistic</u> walk and relationship with the Lord." Think closely with this woman; she had used, or learned to use, prayer as a <u>realistic</u> way to deal with life in the oh-so-daily. Prayer is not only a healthy discipline or a soft place to fall. To pray without ceasing means to pray as a realistic way to handle whatever life brings! "Pray without ceasing", means to live by a schedule that allows prayer to be consistent as well as being impromptu.

Occasionally I'm asked the question, "What about fasting?" Is prayer and fasting something reserved only for Biblical times? We live in fast moving days. We live by hurried schedules. Is it possible for modern day Christians to truly fast and pray? Yes, if priorities are in order. Fasting was never designed to be a parade of piety. Those who fast as a credential of spirituality are misusing the whole idea of fasting. Fasting is simply a discipline whereby you concentrate upon something more important than eating. Fasting and praying are not a form of "sanctified" abuse, but they are a means of removing distractions in favor of concentrating on what is paramount. Though more often than not, prayer and fasting involves abstinence of more things than food alone. Whatever the nature or duration of the fast, the object is to establish a concentration on prayer that cannot be accomplished otherwise. To pray without ceasing is to possess a worshipping, grateful, intercessory, imploring tongue.

The genuinely prayerful tongue is a <u>reminiscent</u> tongue. In that same segment of scripture where Paul was led to admonish the Thessalonian believers, he said, "Rejoice always…" and then, one sentence removed, he says, "…in everything give thanks, for this is God's will for you" (1 Thessalonians 5:16-18). This is not just a good option. Neither is it just advisable. This is God's will concerning you. It is healthy, it is wholesome, and it is God's will that you learn to give thanks in everything. In other words, we are challenged to live in a state of grateful reminiscence.

Now I think there are some other lessons at this point for us to learn as well. There are no Christians who are joyful, pleasant people and at the same time are unloving, unholy, and ungrateful. To be ungrateful, to be unholy, and to be unloving is to pave the road toward being unpleasant and being defeated. And so to give thanks in everything; this is God's will concerning us. Another lesson we need to learn is that you can deal with failure and fear by concentrating on past victories. That's pragmatic. It is not an invitation to <u>live in the past</u>. It is an invitation to be <u>encouraged by the past</u>. Another thing to learn is the discipline of gratitude. Someone may want to say to me at this point, "I just have to admit to you, I'm not a big thanker. I find it awkward to look a person straight in the eye and say thank you." Well, I have two words for you. Get unawkward! If you have to learn to sing it, if you have to learn how to put it in poetry, if you have to learn how to write it in a letter, allow yourself to get unawkward! It is God's will concerning us that we be thankful. Having a capacity for reminiscence, we can learn to overflow with praise, lest we take God's goodness for granted.

There is still another lesson to be learned about the praying, imploring tongue. It is a <u>repentant</u> tongue. In Luke 18, Jesus told a parable of two men who went up to the temple to pray, one a Pharisee, one a publican. Now the Pharisees had a practice, of repeating certain prayers on a daily basis. They would say things like, "I thank God I am not like other people are; I am thankful I'm not a Gentile; I thank God I am not a woman; I thank God I am not a slave." As an aside, isn't it interesting; among the first converts to Christianity in Europe were a Gentile, a woman, and a slave! So here in the Temple is one who prays as other Pharisees did. I thank God I'm not a Gentile, I thank God I'm not a woman, I thank God I'm not a slave, and he looked at the publican and said, "I thank God I'm not like this." Then the publican, who would not even lift up his eyes unto Heaven, pounded upon his chest and said, "Oh, God be merciful to me the sinner" (Luke 18:13). And Jesus concluded, "I tell you, that man went to his home justified rather than the other" (Luke 18:14). Part of our problem is the Pharisee's problem. We rationalize our behavior, defend ourselves in arrogance and self-pity and have not learned to say openly, "Oh God be merciful to me, a sinner." If the imploring tongue speaks any language, it speaks <u>fluent</u> <u>repentance</u>!

In the 9th and 10th chapters of the Old Testament book of Ezra, there is an extremely insightful study about this matter of a repentant tongue. The setting of this book was at the time in Israel's history after they had been taken away into bondage by the Babylonians. They spent seventy years in bondage, until the Persians had overrun the Babylonians and had allowed the Jews to return to the land of their heritage. As Zerubbabel led these Jews back to Jerusalem they had begun to rebuild life in and about that capital city. Of course, one of the first things they did was to rebuild the temple that the Babylonians had destroyed. Ezra the priest and scribe came soon thereafter and helped to reinstitute worship in that temple. In a matter of days after Ezra had returned, there were certain leaders of Judah, "princes" as the Scripture calls them, who reported to him that in the short time these Jewish people had returned they had already become involved in sin and overt disobedience. Hardly believable that people who had suffered so much because of their previous sin would return to the very same sin, but they did precisely that! They had compromised themselves with pagans. They had intermarried with unbelievers. They had done the very things they had been instructed not to do. The Bible then recounts Ezra's imploring reaction:

> "And at the evening sacrifice I rose up from my heaviness and having rent my garment and mantle, I fell upon my knees, I spread out my hands to the Lord my God, and I said, Oh my God, I am shamed and I blush to lift up my face to you my God; for our iniquities are increased

over our head, and our trespass is grown up unto the heavens" (Ezra 9:5, KJV).

There follows the self-emptying words of an honest, repentant man. This open confession was made in the presence of his peers; as he confessed his own sin and the sin of his people. The 10th chapter begins then with the people's response. "Now when Ezra had prayed, and when he had confessed, weeping and casting himself down before the house of God, there assembled unto him out of Israel a very great congregation of men and women and children: for the people wept very sore" (Ezra 10:1, KJV). There is a magnetism, a stirring inspiration for people when they recognize those who are in spiritual leadership are serious about the business of confession and repentance. There is something about the repentant voice that causes others to follow the example. As a result of Ezra's imploring prayer, there was purification, a purging that took place among God's repentant people.

A prayerful tongue is not only a repentant tongue; it is a <u>reconciling</u> tongue as well. Unquestionably, the scripture clearly teaches us that we experience forgiveness as we offer it. Jesus said, "If you will forgive men their trespasses, your Father in Heaven will also forgive your trespasses" (Matthew 6:14, KJV). That is not to say that God forgives contingent on something we do. God forgives because it is His nature to forgive. He does not function on a contingency that you and I offer. However, we do not <u>experience</u> forgiveness unless there is a forgiving spirit within us. Sad, isn't it, God has secured our forgiveness; it is a settled transaction, and our arrogance can deprive us of experiencing it! Such is the travesty in many a church pew, choir loft, yes, and even a pulpit!

Any consideration of the prayerful tongue would be incomplete without the realization it is a <u>responsive</u> tongue. That is, it seeks to intercede because it is sensitive to the needs and the joys of others. In order for us to have a compassionate tongue, and in order for us to be a responsive intercessor, there are three things we must do. In the first place, <u>we must listen</u>. There is no way that you and I can be genuine intercessors, and pray with sensitivity without listening first. Listen to God, listen to others, and listen to what they have to say. Secondly, <u>we must love</u>. "Bear one another's burdens and thereby fulfill the law of Christ" (Galatians 6:2). And what's the law of Christ? To love one another as he loves us! Thirdly, <u>we must linger</u>. As we have already learned; we are to pray without ceasing. It's that simple. We must pray it through. We can't stop praying one day too soon if we are going to be a responsive intercessor.

Now may I share an exciting thought? Jesus Christ is the same yesterday, today, forever. Whatever your circumstance, you have available to you a Savior who never changes. He's always merciful, always responsive, and always ready for you. And you have a tongue by which you can address Him. What do you need to talk to Him about today? Do you need to accept Christ as your personal Savior and make Him the Lord of your life? Do you need to confess sin? Do you need to acknowledge guilt? Do you need to ask someone to forgive you? Do you need to express overdue gratitude to someone? Allow that tongue of yours to make a difference. Remember the power of life and death is in <u>your tongue</u>!

> "When we depend on organization, we get what organization can do;
> We depend on education, we get what education can do;
> When we depend on man, we get what man can do;
> But when we depend on prayer, we get what God can do."
>
> Nick Harrison, *Magnificent Prayer*,
> (Zondervan, 2001), 196

Chapter 5

The Acid Tongue

"They have sharpened their tongues like a serpent; adders' poison is under their lips" (Psalm 140:3, KJV).

The Awesome Power of the Tongue

Several years ago one of the most genuine, down to earth, preachers of the gospel I have ever known was buried in the red dirt of his native Alabama. He was an uncomplicated and plain man. He was equally plain spoken. He was what we would call a working man's pastor; a good old fashioned Baptist preacher. He preached plain sermons. He used graphic, simple, down to earth illustrations about his memories of boyhood days on the farm; and he communicated well. He died of cancer. But long before cancer took his life, something killed what was inside of him. What was that? It was purely and simply a bold faced lie that was spread through a network of gossips. By the time the lie had fully traveled the network he became indefensibly guilty. He never recovered. Oh yes, he moved on to other churches and other ministries but it was never the same. He had been fired from his church. Of course, the culprit lie was discovered some time after he had been dismissed. It was found that the whole thing had its origin in a convenient lie. It was what is sometimes called a little "white" lie. But I want you to know that sometimes the blackest results can come from the whitest of lies. It was told by a family member who had slipped away from the bedside of a dying relative, to take a joy ride in a friend's new car, who wanted to cover her irresponsible tracks. So she authored a story about the preacher who never came to visit the dying patient. Of course he did come. He came during the joy ride, but after the lie was discovered the damage had been done. The pastor had been shamed. His family had been embarrassed. He had to move on to other places. It hardly seems possible that such a lie could be so destructive, but it was the match that set afire the ready underbrush of gossip!

We often think our caustic tongues are our blunt and courageous tongues. The tongue that is used to even the score, or to put those people who are out of place in their places, is not courageous. Sarcastic tongues are not as clever as we may think they are. When we resort to the acid tongue we are not nearly as courageous as we think. Actually, more than anything else, we are just cunning snipers who happen to have good verbal marksmanship. We know how to bull's-eye our targets.

Little wonder when James came to write his five chapter letter he put so much emphasis on the tongue. This James is widely thought to be the half-brother of our Lord. What James wrote is what we call a General Epistle. It was a letter meant for all Christians living in his day. And as the Holy Spirit has preserved it there is a sense it is very much meant for us. The Holy Spirit seems to give James an emphasis, first of all, on the size of the tongue. You might wonder why. And I suppose those believers who first received his letter wondered why. After all, if eternity is at stake, if Christ's reputation and message is at stake, if world evangelization is at stake, if eternal truth is at stake, why would so much emphasis be placed on a little instrument that is attached to your jawbone? Obviously, the size of the tongue is deceptive, considering its potential. In James 3:3-5, he writes about the size of the tongue:

> "Now if we put the bits into the horses' mouths so that they will obey us, we direct their entire

body as well. Look at the ships also, though they are so great and are driven by strong winds, are still directed by a very small rudder wherever the inclination of the pilot desires."

Like a piece of metal placed in the mouth of a horse, when pulled to the left, or pulled to the right, or pulled directly back, controls that huge muscular animal. Just like a rudder, small when compared to the size of the sails, can turn a whole ship even though it is driven by a fierce wind; simply because the pilot moves it. Similarly, the tongue is little, but it boasts great things. It can afford to boast great things. Though it is small it can accomplish big results. "See how great a forest is set aflame by such a small fire" (James 3:5)! Only a spark is needed and you can have a forest fire. That's the emphasis of James. The tongue by comparison is small. It is a tiny member, but like other tiny objects it can afford to boast about great accomplishments.

Now James moves to the <u>significance</u> of the tongue. Consider verse 6. "And the tongue is a fire; the very world of iniquity… (meaning, it is in itself an evil world.) …the tongue is set among our members as that which defiles the entire body, and sets on fire the course of our life and is set on fire by hell." Note the significant dimensions of the tongues' impact. It is like unto an evil world. It defiles the whole body; not just the lips and the mouth. Furthermore, it actually can determine the course of nature or the outcome of history. It is a fire started in the pits of hell itself! That is significant!

From the size of the tongue to the significance of the tongue, James then comes to the <u>sins</u> of the tongue. In verses 7-10 there are some general references about the tongue and its misuse. Before going any further we need to underscore some positive contributions of the tongue. It is capable of doing glorious things; praising God, talking to the Almighty Sovereign of the universe. It is capable of bringing laughter. The tongue is able to give comfort. It is capable of bearing a witness. The tongue is able to bring joy. The tongue is capable of delivering life-altering encouragement. To be complete, however, we must consider the sins of the tongue. In an effort to simplify the matter, there are four basic sins of the tongue. Those basic sins are gossip, profanity, deceit, and vengeance. Most any misuse of the tongue can be categorized in one of those four areas:

1. Gossip: spreading malicious rumors or exaggerations
2. Profanity: denigrating persons, usurping God's exclusive authority, trivializing the Sacred
3. Deceit: distorting or denying the truth
4. Vengeance: hatred linked to bitterness and hostility

But James is interested in more than just simply analyzing the sins of the tongue. He is greatly interested in the <u>submission</u> of the tongue. Why? For the tongue is not something you and I can easily control. Oh, for short periods of time, or on given occasions, we may be able to control the tongue. But in the main, the tongue must be controlled for us. Therefore the Christian must bring the tongue to a place of submission so that the indwelling Holy Spirit can override the power of one's emotions or the circumstance in which we find ourselves. Looking again at James 3:1, "Let not many of you become teachers, my brethren, knowing that as such, we will incur a stricter judgment". James is saying do not seek a high profile. The old principle, in Luke 12:48, applies, "For unto whomsoever much is given, of him shall be much required"(KJV). Rightfully, those who represent the Gospel, are to be looked to for an example and they are highly accountable. So, do not seek the spotlight. There is enough accountability without seeking it. To whom much is given, much is required. That's the emphasis.

James moves on to verse 2, "For we all stumble in many ways." All of us stumble. We have our moments when we are at our dedicated, consecrated best; at our prayerful best; our meticulous best; but even at our best we will stumble. There are times when people will misunderstand you. They will not comprehend what you are about. It is risky to be a Christian in a non-Christian world. You will stumble even at your best. "For we all stumble in many ways." Read on, "If anyone does not stumble in what he says…" (meaning, in his choice of words), "…he is a perfect man able to bridle the whole body as well" (James 3:2). Got it? If you can bridle your choice of words; if you can bring your tongue under God's control, then you are indeed on your way to a real measure of maturity. You will be seen as trustworthy. In fact, if your tongue is under God's control, generally speaking, the whole of your personality is under control. If your tongue is not under God's control then you cannot boast of your maturity. You are as unpredictable as a child. You are more emotional than reasonable. It is true that "as a man thinks in his heart, so he is" (Proverbs 23:7, KJV). But it is equally true; as one speaks with the tongue so is his heart revealed!

Now let's single out one particular sin of the tongue, namely, gossip. Gossip is the language of the acid tongue. It would seem most dictionaries define "acid" in terms of bitterness, a sharp, biting taste. Acid is corrosive to metal. Acid rain is caused by pollution in the air. Acid is equated with a sour substance. All of these statements serve well to describe the tongue of gossip. If any of us really want to get our acid tongue under Divine control we would do well to focus attention on James 3:8. The verse reads, "But no one can tame the tongue." It does not mean we cannot submit it for control; that we <u>can</u> do. But we cannot by our own dent of effort to bring the tongue under control. "It is a restless evil." It is the match that lights a wildfire!

Take note of three character traits that James gives about the tongue. First, it is <u>unmanageable</u>. No man can tame it! It is uncontrolled. Second, it is an <u>unpredictable</u> tongue. It is a restless evil. It does not follow any rules of conduct. It does not follow principles. Third, it is an <u>unmerciful</u> tongue. It is "full of deadly poison." The word translated "poison" is a Greek word used several ways in the New Testament. For instance, James uses the word in chapter 5:2, when speaking about wealth that is an obsession, a distraction from one's relationship to God. "Your riches have rotted." The word translated "poison" in one place is translated "rotted" here. It's a word that refers to infection, leading to serious disease. The passage, goes on to say in verse 3, that their gold and silver is rusted. In this instance the word refers to deterioration. In another occasion, the acid tongue is like an infection corrupting the body. We are reminded that the words of an acid tongue are like the venom of a snake or the poison in food or drink. So here is the emphasis: the tongue can infect; the tongue can deteriorate; the tongue can annihilate. It can corrupt and destroy. It can eat away so as to destroy a person, like infection destroys a physical body. Or it can kill a reputation, divide a church and condemn before there is a verdict. The tongue, then, when used for acidic gossip, is uncontrolled, it is unpredictable, and it is unmerciful. Even masked and diluted with sarcasm, the acid tongue is still a deadly poison!

What does God's writer have to say about the submission of the tongue? How do we bring our tongue to the capability of praising God, and witnessing Christ: and bringing comfort and joy and laughter? We need to return to the very sentence that introduces James' treatise on the tongue. "If anyone does not stumble in what he says, he is a perfect man, able to bridle the whole body as well" (James 3:2). There is then the need for Christians to recognize that this tongue of ours needs to be submitted to the Lordship of Christ if we have any hope of maturity.

There are some questions to be faced by any Christian who is serious about developing a tongue under Godly control. These are legitimate questions that deserve honest answers.

1. Is my tongue serving my character or primarily serving my emotions? We are emotional creatures. That cannot be changed. God made us that way. It is not wrong for

us to have emotional responses. There are some things that endanger us and we should have a healthy fear of them. There are some things that make us overflow with joy; and we should welcome them. There are some things that stimulate us and others that cause us to be pensive. What we have to ask is not, "Am I emotional or am I in control of my emotions?" The issue is, "Is my tongue more the servant of my character or my emotions?" Our character is molded by upbringing, godly influences, by the Bible, and prayer. Our tongues are always ready to give voice to our emotions. The question, then is not can our tongues get emotional, rather, is our character more in charge of our tongues, or are our emotions?

2. Am I telling what I know to be true or only what I have heard? It is probably far more entertaining to tell what you have heard than it is to do the research and find out the facts. You will have to acknowledge that is true. Unfortunately, it makes us more exciting to other people if we can tell what we have heard and not be held accountable for knowing it. If you really want to deal with someone when they begin to tell you what they have heard; you can say, "How did you learn that? Are you positive that's true?" You'll probably find your conversation will be rather brief because there are other people all too ready to listen to the gossip.

3. Will the impact of what I say be worth what caused me to say it? Sometimes we want to speak all too quickly. So

we must ask will the effect of what I am about to say be worth what caused me to say it?

4. This question is no less important: Would I say later what I'm about to say right now? Anyone who is in public life will be the first to tell you; don't say now what you would not say later. After preaching a sermon on the tongue some years ago, I was asked, "How did you know so much about my tongue?" I responded, "Well, I know quite a lot about my own." Is my character so small or my spirit so shallow that I cannot refuse my emotional impulses to do most of the talking? Sometimes the best response or statement you can make is what your character has to say rather than your feelings. In fact, your character can be far more eloquent than what your words might be.

5. Do I want to live with the reputation my tongue is making for me? Do I like the idea of being known as a hothead? Do I want to be known as a sorehead? Do I want to be known as a gossip? Do you like the reputation that your tongue is making for you? It's a good question. You really ought to answer it.

6. In defending my integrity or in destroying somebody else's, is my tongue degrading my Lord's integrity in the process? To bear Jesus' name is as high a privilege there is; to degrade His reputation is a serious proposition.

7. Are my temper and my tongue as saved as my eternal spirit? Is that a strange way to put it? Consider this, if you're saved you're saved all together. In fact, the Bible says you're saved to the uttermost (Hebrews 7:25, KJV,

author's paraphrase). Understand me; I'm not only talking about what God has accomplished in the death, burial, and resurrection of Jesus. But what impact and effect has all that had upon the use of the tongue? I submit to you that it may be a strange confrontation; but it may be that some have been saved 25 years, 30 years, 15 years, 40 years, and may find themselves at the place where, for the first time, this question has been considered: Have I ever submitted my temper and my tongue to Jesus Christ to save and give new birth? I suggest to you, here at the conclusion of this chapter, this may be a crossroads opportunity for you to exchange an old tongue for a new one.

> "Be careful of your thoughts;
> they may quickly become words."
>
> A Church Bulletin Board,
> Warren, PA, July 2012

Chapter 6

The Positive Tongue

"Let no corrupt communication proceed out of your mouth but that which is good to the use of edifying, that it may minister grace to the hearers" (Ephesians 4:29, KJV).

There's a very old and a time worn fable that you probably have heard but it may have been so long ago that you might not even recognize it. So, you may want to hear it again. It's the story of a monk who joined an order of silence. The agreement was that he would spend ten years in total silence. At the end of the ten years he would be allowed to speak three words. And then he would repeat the cycle. So, after he spent ten years in utter silence, he came before his superiors at the end of the ten years and they said to him, "You may speak your three words." And he said, "Food, too cold." They said, "Well, perhaps we could do something about that. We'll see to it that you'll get some warmer food in the future." So the monk spent the next ten years in utter silence; didn't say a word. He came back at the end of ten years and appeared before his superiors and they said, "Now you may speak your three words." He answered, "Bed, too hard." And so they said, "All right, we can do something about that. We can give you a softer mattress; make it a little more comfortable." The monk then spent the next ten years in utter silence. For thirty years he lived in utter silence except for speaking six words. At the end of the third segment of ten years he came before the authorities and they asked, "Now you have your three words, what are they?" He said, "I quit." One of his superiors responded, "Well, you might as well. You've been here for thirty years and haven't done anything but complain the whole time you've been here!"

Most of us would be rather delighted if it could be said that in thirty years we only spoke eight words of complaint, but that's not the issue. The issue is not how <u>many</u> negative or critical words we speak. The issue is the condition of the heart that beats <u>beneath</u> the words we speak. The fact of the matter is these tongues of ours are only an instrument that expresses what lies beneath. It's our spirit; the inner person that really determines what we say. Jesus said it best. You'll find His take on the matter in the 7th chapter of the Gospel of Mark. Let's focus again upon what Jesus said about the inner spirit; that which is inside us that really causes us to have the negative, snide, and acid-like tongue some of us have. In effect, Jesus said to these traditional Jewish people, "You have become so hide bound to your traditions that you are bypassing the law of God. In fact, you have become so obsessed with such things as the washing of cups and plates, to prevent yourself from becoming contaminated, that you are ignoring the law of God." He used an illustration. "Moses taught you to honor your father and mother. And you have instead said to your needy parents or to those who have come to that stage in life wherein they need your help and your support, 'Corban!' (meaning 'the gifts that we would have given you we have really given to God). Therefore I am relieved of any responsibility for you.' And Jesus continued, don't you see, in your tradition you have ignored and disobeyed the Law of God" (Mark 7:10-13, author's paraphrase). So his disciples asked him more about that illustration and about his teaching; to which Jesus replied, "There is nothing outside the man which can defile him if it goes into him; but the things which proceed out of the man are what defile the man"(Mark 7:15). Listen to Jesus enlarge the subject a bit further:

"That which proceeds out of the man, that is what defiles the man. For from within, out of the heart of men, proceed evil thoughts, fornications, thefts, murders, adulteries, deeds of coveting and wickedness, as well as deceit, sensuality, envy, slander, pride and foolishness. All these evil things proceed from within and defile the man" (Mark 7:20-23).

That which emits from your tongue, that is negative, critical, cynical, skeptical, and snide really has its birth, not in the back of your throat, but in the depth of your heart.

When we come to occasions with emphases on the home and family, there are certain classic passages in the Bible to which we naturally turn. At this moment there is one I find turning over in my head. It's the 31st chapter of Proverbs wherein the virtuous woman is described. In particular, the sentence that strikes home with me is this one: "She opens her mouth in wisdom, and the teaching of kindness is on her tongue" (Proverbs 31:26). In the Hebrew language the word translated "kindness" can also be translated "loyalty". It carries with it the idea of being supportive, standing along beside, giving to someone your positive support. If you translate that verse in language we better understand and use today, it is said of the virtuous, godly woman: "When she speaks she says wise things because her tongue lives by the law of the positive." Got it? When this woman speaks she says wise things, because her tongue lives by the law of the positive.

If you take the time to look up the word "positive" you'll find there are numerous synonyms. You will find words like definite, affirmative, convinced, and exact. As the list expands there are still more words synonymous to the word positive. In fact, I found five such words I will use in this chapter to explore the positive tongue. Here they are: <u>confident</u>, <u>firm</u>, <u>reassuring</u>, <u>disarming</u>, and <u>noble</u>. Those words can examine our tongues for us and answer questions like, "How positive am I when I speak? Do I strike a positive note or am I given to negativity? Is what I have to say worth hearing, because I am positive of it and because I instill the positive? After my contribution to the conversation is there any reason to hope?

Take notice, if you have a positive tongue you have a <u>confident tongue</u>. The meaning of the word positive, in some instances, is confident, sure, definite. So if you have a positive tongue you may mark it down, it will be a confident tongue. For Christians it means we have a confidence about our relationship to the Lord. It means we have a confidence about the very nature of the Bible. It means we speak with the confidence and force of what God has promised. In 1 Corinthians 14, you will find more insight into what it means to speak with a confident tongue. The emphasis in that chapter is not so much upon the tongue of speech as it is the tongue of worship, but the principle still applies.

> "But now, brethren, if I come to you speaking in tongues, what will I profit you unless I speak to you either by way of revelation or of

> knowledge or of prophecy or of teaching" (1 Corinthians 14:6)?

The point is, whether you are speaking in an ecstatic tongue, a worship tongue, or talking with a scholarly tongue: of what consequence is it, if it is not distinct, speaking clearly and plainly the truth of the Gospel?

In sentences that follow, Paul uses the battlefield for an example of disaster when orders are unclear. He describes a bugle blasting out uncertain sounds, resulting in confusion. Are the troops to charge or are they to retreat? Is the enemy attacking from the flank or are they coming head on? The issue is not troop strength or adequate weaponry, but botched communication! "So also you, unless you utter by the tongue speech that is clear, how will it be known what is spoken? For you will be speaking into the air" (1 Corinthians 14:9). Of what consequence is it if you don't know what you are talking about? Or what if you know the truth but relate that truth apologetically or timidly? It's not a matter of being brash and smug; it is rather an issue of being Biblically and experientially confident.

Moving to something the apostle Paul wrote to Timothy we read:

> "For I am mindful of the sincere faith within you, which first dwelt in your grandmother Lois and your mother Eunice, and I am sure that it is in you as well. For this reason I remind you to kindle afresh the gift of God which is in you

through the laying on of my hands" (2 Timothy 1:5-6).

"God doesn't want us to be shy with His gifts, but bold, loving, and sensible. So don't be embarrassed to speak up for our Master or for me, His prisoner. Take your share of suffering for the message along with the rest of us. We can only keep going, after all, by the power of God, who first saved us and then called us to this holy work. We had nothing to do with it. It was all His idea, a gift prepared for us in Jesus long before we knew anything about it. But we know it now. Since the appearance of our Savior, nothing could be plainer; death defeated, life vindicated in a steady blaze of light, all through the work of Jesus. This is the Message I've been set apart to proclaim as preacher, emissary, and teacher. It's also the cause of all this trouble I'm in. But I have no regrets. I couldn't be more sure of my ground – the One I've trusted in can take care of what he's trusted me to do right to the end" (2 Timothy 1:7-12, The Message).

A positive tongue in a Christian's mouth will, of necessity, be a confident tongue; confident of one's relationship to Christ; confident that what is committed to him he will preserve unto His return; confident that what God says I can count upon;

confident that when I speak in God's behalf and I speak it truthfully, God will verify it!

Let me issue a warning. There is a world of difference between being confident and being an overbearing, arrogant know-it-all. I have been around some Christians who speak with what is apparently a confident tongue, but the more I listen the greater the impression I have that the confidence is in themselves. There is a certain arrogance in the voice, if put to words would say, "After I speak, there is nothing else to be said." That mentality is one that provides kindling for tongues to start fires! Paul's example of confidence is the one to be followed: "I know whom I have believed and am convinced that He is able to guard what I have entrusted to <u>Him</u>" (2 Timothy 1:12).

The positive tongue is, likewise, <u>a firm tongue</u>. Someone who is positive is firm. It is not just a matter of being confident but speaking with firmness. For 4 ½ years I attended a military high school. In that setting there is still a language of firmness to be heard on every hand. Close order drills and the manual of arms are inseparably linked to words like, "Attention!" (pronounced, "Ten-hutt!") and "Present Arms!" (pronounced, pree-sent-haams!) Firmness is attached to those words, because behind those words there is authority. Such is the firmness of a Christian's positive tongue. There is Biblical authority and the witness of God's Holy Spirit that serve as the foundation of words spoken with a positive tongue.

There is still another dimension inherent to the positive tongue. That dimension is reassurance. A positive tongue is <u>a reassuring tongue</u>. One of my favorite Bible passages is the 3rd chapter of Colossians. In that chapter, we learn specifics about how Christians can, and should, reassure one another:

> "So as those who have been chosen of God, holy and beloved, put on a heart of compassion, kindness, humility, gentleness and patience; bearing with one another and forgiving each other, whoever has a complaint against anyone; just as the lord forgave you, so also should you. Beyond all these things, put on love, which is the perfect bond of unity. Let the peace of Christ rule in your hearts, to which indeed you were called in one body; and be thankful. Let the word of Christ richly dwell within you with all wisdom teaching and admonishing one another with psalms and hymns and spiritual songs, singing with thankfulness in your hearts to God" (Colossians 3:12-16).

Encourage one another. Admonish one another. Share with each other the inner Spirit of grace and love. Speak reassurance with a positive tongue!

Canadian Geese make an interesting kind of formation when they fly. They fly in a "V" formation that greatly boosts their efficiency. The online encyclopedia, Wikipedia, suggests that flying in that formation with 25 birds, each bird reduces the drag on it by 65% and increases its range by 71%. The geese even have a rotation plan whereby they take turns at the front and on the tips of the formation, equalizing flight fatigue. They know they can do better together than alone. I guess we ought to learn something from the birds!

The Lord Jesus conceived what we call the Church, or the fellowship of His body. He figured we would need each other to reassure, to uplift, encourage, offer help and hope to one another. We should do together what we cannot accomplish alone. We are told to admonish one another, correct one another, speaking the truth in love. We ought not to be so stingy with our words of reassurance. We ought to say those kinds of things that lift the spirit. When you walk away from that Bible Study you attend, what do you say to your teacher, if anything? At the close of a worship service and when you encounter a choir member what do you say to that choir member? How long has it been since you sat down and wrote a note to someone and said, "I thank you and I thank <u>God</u> for you."? Perhaps you secretly lament the fact that people do not compliment you, or that you go unnoticed. When did <u>you</u> last pick up the phone or send a text message for no other reason than to specifically thank a believer for his contribution to your life? Who knows, you may be God's provision for their feelings of neglect and sagging self-worth!

It means a great deal to me when people take the time to speak to me following a sermon I have preached. I am told some people feel awkward about those encounters. Perhaps they have heard in somebody's conference or off someone's cuff that you are not supposed to "enjoy" a sermon. I've actually been greeted after a service with, "I know I'm not supposed to enjoy a sermon," followed by an attempt to find some other words that will not be the wrong thing to say. Just say it like you feel it. If you enjoy it, enjoy it. Just say it.

In honesty, the encouragements I value most are from my ministerial peers. I appreciate what these fellow ministers have to say to me. Some of them do not say much, or say it often. Some of them are specific about a truth which applied to them and they say it immediately. Still others reserve their comment to a private moment the next day. Now and then, the comment is written in a note. In an e-mailer's and text messenger's world, it is refreshing to hear from someone who knows the art and worth of handwritten notes. And then there are times when someone cares enough for me to correct me, and they don't do it anonymously! All such communication from my fellow believers is significant to me.

Admittedly, there is one person, above all others, whose opinion I value. When my wife says I'm on target, I know I am on target. When she has little or nothing to say, I just as well not ask!

Men, listen up, of all the people around her life do you realize that the one voice your wife wants to hear more than any other voice, offering her commendation and encouragement, is yours? And don't join with that mythical husband who said, "I don't need to tell her I love her. I told her thirty years ago and I'll let her know if I ever change my mind." And ladies, they may handle it awkwardly, even act like it doesn't matter, but there is one loving voice, more than any that a man wants to hear and that is his bride's! And parents, while we are at it, here's something written for you. How long has it been since you said to your children, "I'm so proud of you I could burst!" This is not to endorse the philosophy of surrounding a child with an exclusive diet of success. Giving a Most Valuable Player trophy to every team member just for showing up actually reduces excellence to the ordinary. Remember, "It takes 100 at-a-boys to balance with one criticism!" Let young people choose their own best promises for fulfillment and then become their best fan! And while we are on the subject, some of you are adult children. You're not small children anymore, you're not even teenagers, you are now grown men and women. Your parents taught you to be courteous, to be gracious and appreciative to neighbors, school teachers, even distant relatives. But let me ask, why on earth are you not more appreciative to your own parents? One of the most hurtful things to a parent's heart is to have a child you have taught to be courteous and appreciative to other people; but that child seldom looks into your eyes and simply says, "Thank you, mom. Thank you, dad." We need to learn again that deep in our hearts, the people from whom we want to hear most, are those who are dearest to us. At your house and at the church house should be the most likely places to hear the sounds of a positive tongue.

A brief observation: A positive tongue is <u>a disarming tongue</u>. Proverbs 15:1-2 says "A gentle answer turns away wrath, but a harsh word stirs up anger. The tongue of the wise makes knowledge acceptable, but the mouth of fools spouts folly." The King James version describes the disarming tongue as "a soft answer". That should not be mistaken for a coward's reply or a weak response. In a tense moment or a heated exchange, words laced with grace rob anger of its satisfaction. See if reading the latter part of Romans 12 gives added meaning to the inability of anger to handle grace. The apostle Paul quotes Deuteronomy 32:25, saying vengeance is God's responsibility. He says, if you will answer those who are hostile to you with generosity and grace, something will happen to the top of their head; something like hot coals landing there!

There is one last quality about a positive tongue we could do well to note. A positive tongue is <u>a noble tongue</u>. If you are looking for a noble tongue you will find it on the high road. The high road is found on the map of those whose hearts are under the Holy Spirit's control. The Bible tells us we have the potential of the mind of Christ. In other words, thinking like Jesus, we follow the high road. There is a great passage in God's Word that will put you on the high road:

> "Finally brethren, whatever is true, whatever is honorable, whatever is right, whatever is pure, whatever is lovely, whatever is of good repute, if there is any excellence and if anything worthy praise, dwell on these things" (Philippians 4:8).

The Positive Confession Movement, by the way, uses that text as one of their favorites. But there is more than positive thinking involved. Selective moments to choose positive thoughts will not keep us on the high road. Yielding our minds to the over-ruling mind of Christ will keep us on the noble road rather than just choosing it from time to time. That's why Paul says, "<u>dwell</u> on these things".

If we have a "walk with the Lord" it will be on the high road because that's the only road He walks. There the language of the positive tongue is the official language of the realm.

> "If the whole world followed you –
> Followed you to the letter,
> Would it be a nobler world,
> All deceit and falsehood hurled
> From it altogether,
> Malice, selfishness, and lust,
> Banished from beneath the crust,
> Covering human hearts from view –
> Tell me, if followed you,
> Would the world be better?"

William Bennett, *The Book of Virtues*, (Simon and Schuster, 1993), 644

Chapter 7

The Encouraging Tongue

"For God has not given us the spirit of fear; but of power and of love, and of a sound mind" (2 Timothy 1:7).

This is a chapter about encouragement. We can live physically without food for unbelievable periods of time. We cannot live without water but for a few days. But there are times in our lives when we cannot live another minute without hope; more than water, more than food. To be responsible for voicing hope is fundamental to a Christian's witness in an often-charred and smoldering world.

Dr. R. G. Lee, now with the Lord, was pastor of the Bellevue Baptist Church in Memphis, Tennessee for many years and was considered a prince of preachers. After speaking to a conference of pastors, he was asked, "Dr. Lee, now that you are retired, what would you do differently if you could start over again?" Without hesitation, the seasoned, tried and proven pastor answered, "If I could do it over again, I would preach more on encouragement." Though I am not in a league with Dr. Lee, I tend to agree, for I too, would be inclined to preach more on encouragement.

There was an occasion during their first missionary journey, when Paul and Barnabas arrived in Pisidia and went to the synagogue there. After the worship period was over they were asked to share what was on their hearts. In the book of Acts, chapter 13, we see how this setting unfolds and how it applies to ourselves. Remember, we are thinking about encouragement and the absolute necessity of it. The Bible tells us that Paul and Barnabas had gone to Cyprus, preached across the island, being met with both opposition and belief. Then having left Cyprus, that was Barnabas' home, they went to Perga, Pamphylia. Verse 14 continues:

> "But going on from Perga, they arrived at Pisidian Antioch, and on the Sabbath day they went into the synagogue and sat down." They were not guest preachers, they were unexpected visitors. "After the reading of the Law and the Prophets the synagogue officials sent to them, saying, 'Brethren, if you have any word of exhortation for people, say it" (Acts 13:15).

I have no idea what these who led the synagogue knew. I have no clue what problems or burdens there were, but there were some, that's for sure. The service now being over, the synagogue leaders sent to Paul and Barnabas and said, "If you have any word of exhortation for the people, come and say it." The word translated "exhortation", (parakletos), is derived from the word meaning "comfort". It's a word that implies <u>encouragement and hope</u>. "If you have a word of encouragement," they said, "if you've got something to say in the realm of hope, please say it." Now at that particular point my interest perks. I really want to know what Paul and Barnabas are going to say. They are asked to use their tongues for encouragement in ways that will bless these folks in that realm of their lives.

'Paul stood up, and motioning with his hand said, 'Men of Israel, and you who fear God, listen'" (v.16). Give audience, in other words, give me your ear. If he were using language we use today, he would say, "Listen up! Pay attention!" Then he begins to speak about things that would direct these people toward hope. He reaches back into Jewish history and reminds

The Awesome Power of the Tongue

This is a chapter about encouragement. We can live physically without food for unbelievable periods of time. We cannot live without water but for a few days. But there are times in our lives when we cannot live another minute without hope; more than water, more than food. To be responsible for voicing hope is fundamental to a Christian's witness in an often-charred and smoldering world.

Dr. R. G. Lee, now with the Lord, was pastor of the Bellevue Baptist Church in Memphis, Tennessee for many years and was considered a prince of preachers. After speaking to a conference of pastors, he was asked, "Dr. Lee, now that you are retired, what would you do differently if you could start over again?" Without hesitation, the seasoned, tried and proven pastor answered, "If I could do it over again, I would preach more on encouragement." Though I am not in a league with Dr. Lee, I tend to agree, for I too, would be inclined to preach more on encouragement.

There was an occasion during their first missionary journey, when Paul and Barnabas arrived in Pisidia and went to the synagogue there. After the worship period was over they were asked to share what was on their hearts. In the book of Acts, chapter 13, we see how this setting unfolds and how it applies to ourselves. Remember, we are thinking about encouragement and the absolute necessity of it. The Bible tells us that Paul and Barnabas had gone to Cyprus, preached across the island, being met with both opposition and belief. Then having left Cyprus, that was Barnabas' home, they went to Perga, Pamphylia. Verse 14 continues:

"But going on from Perga, they arrived at Pisidian Antioch, and on the Sabbath day they went into the synagogue and sat down." They were not guest preachers, they were unexpected visitors. "After the reading of the Law and the Prophets the synagogue officials sent to them, saying, 'Brethren, if you have any word of exhortation for people, say it" (Acts 13:15).

I have no idea what these who led the synagogue knew. I have no clue what problems or burdens there were, but there were some, that's for sure. The service now being over, the synagogue leaders sent to Paul and Barnabas and said, "If you have any word of exhortation for the people, come and say it." The word translated "exhortation", (parakletos), is derived from the word meaning "comfort". It's a word that implies <u>encouragement and hope</u>. "If you have a word of encouragement," they said, "if you've got something to say in the realm of hope, please say it." Now at that particular point my interest perks. I really want to know what Paul and Barnabas are going to say. They are asked to use their tongues for encouragement in ways that will bless these folks in that realm of their lives.

'Paul stood up, and motioning with his hand said, 'Men of Israel, and you who fear God, listen'" (v.16). Give audience, in other words, give me your ear. If he were using language we use today, he would say, "Listen up! Pay attention!" Then he begins to speak about things that would direct these people toward hope. He reaches back into Jewish history and reminds them that they were once in bondage in Egypt. God raised up Moses and delivered them from that Egyptian enslavement. He marched them miraculously, dry shod, through the Red Sea to Sinai, and then on to the land of Promise. Then Paul reminds them that, even though they wandered in the wilderness for forty years, due to their disobedience, He did not lose patience with them. "About the time of forty years He suffered their manners in the wilderness" (v.18, KJV). God did indeed, suffer their manners. If you know anything about the history of Israel wandering in that wilderness, having refused to go into the Land of Promise; the Lord God had much to stomach! But, He did not forget them. He did not abandon them. He stuck by them even though they tried His patience. Paul reviews about how God led them in the conquest of Canaan; defeating seven different nations. And because they wanted a king, God raised up kings like David. He mentions David, specifically, who was the king of the greatest of all reputations. And then Paul goes on to say after David's heyday God raised up from his line and lineage, a Savior.

Listen to this, "From the descendants of man, according to promise, God has brought to Israel a Savior, Jesus" (Acts 13:23). Paul goes on and on offering encouragement <u>by way of reminiscence</u>. The Savior God sent died in our stead and God raised Him from the dead. Now focus on Acts 13:38-39:

> "Therefore let it be known to you, brethren, that through Him forgiveness of sins is proclaimed to you and through Him everyone who believes

is freed from all things, from which you could not be freed through the Law of Moses."

The two visiting missionaries were asked to offer encouragement and hope and they did exactly that! Was the synagogue encouraged? I would say they were, for on the next Sabbath day almost the whole city came together to hear the Word of God. Isn't that interesting? On a Sabbath day these two men offered words of encouragement in the synagogue and a week later the place filled up with folks. Do you know why? Because people in <u>that</u> day, as well as <u>this</u> day, need encouragement and hope! Notice the chapter ends with verse 52, "And the disciples were continually filled with joy and with the Holy Spirit." So Paul and Barnabas spoke with tongues of encouragement and the disciples were filled with joy and with the Holy Spirit!

Now let's take this account of Paul and Barnabas' visit in Antioch of Pisidia and see what it says to us. It prompts thoughts about <u>the chemistry of discouragement</u>. What produces discouragement? What brings it about in your life and mine? What are those things that are common to all of us that result in discouragement? If we are going to be encouragers we have to know what we are up against. First, there is <u>guilt</u>. And then there is <u>grief</u>. Beyond grief there is <u>fear</u>. And beyond fear there is <u>anger</u>. Now think with me for a moment. These four things comprise the chemistry that produces discouragement. There are all kinds of things that can discourage us, but these four things are at the very heart and the stem of discouragement: <u>guilt</u>, <u>grief</u>,

The Awesome Power of the Tongue

<u>fear</u>, <u>anger</u>. Remember, if our tongues address discouragement we have to combat these states of mind.

Consider guilt: If there is anything that will discourage you it will be your inability to get away from thoughts of your sin and your guilt. Satan wants to constantly discourage us with the fact that, though forgiven, we have been guilty. When God forgives us through Jesus, we are completely forgiven. In fact the Bible says, "For I will forgive their iniquity and their sin I will remember no more" (Jeremiah 31:34). I don't have that capacity. You don't have that capacity. God does. When God forgives, it's gone as far as He is concerned. Now Satan enters the picture. One thing Satan can never be accused of is stupidity. He knows how to worm his way into our minds and into our spirit whispering, "Yes, God forgave you but, you're just as guilty as you were before. God has forgiven you but I want you to know there are a lot of people who haven't forgotten it." The next thing you know you cannot escape the thought: God has forgiven me, but I'm still held responsible, I still feel guilty. That leads to an inescapable burden, unrest and uncertainty. Satan knows that, so he places before us the very ingredient that mixes into the chemistry of discouragement; namely, guilt. Those who speak with the tongue of encouragement must be merchants of God's forgiveness; God's permanent forgiveness.

Grief also leads to discouragement. I know something about grief. I've been twice widowed. Grief is harsh. You'll never be able, nor should you be able, to forget the one you lost. It's never that you forget it but, you can get better at handling it. But Satan does not want you to handle it. He constantly punctuates the fact that you are lonely, that God has taken someone from you. Paradox though it is, the goodness of God is often best evidenced in the midst of grief. Hence, Satan is ever present to distort and deny the goodness of God and to exaggerate the unfairness of life. Thereby, he can keep us caught in the grips of grief. Extended grief leads to self-pity, despair, anger, and discouragement.

Now fear enters the picture. Satan is a master at threatening us and sowing seeds of fear. We are confronted by things we deem to be greater than we are, stronger than we are, and we are intimidated. At this point we need the reminder of 2 Timothy 1:7, "For God has not given us a spirit of timidity, but of power and love and discipline." God has not given to us the spirit of intimidation, or fear. Left to ourselves, of course; left only to our resources, a lot of things can intimidate us. A person only has to be so much larger than I am and he can intimidate me. There are certain people-types who intimidate you, if you are honest. There are assignments we face and they strike fear. Surrounded by my discomfort zones, am I capable or intimidated? As much as Satan is allowed he will emphasize, underscore, and punctuate fear in your life and mine; so as to discourage us. God did not give to us, by His indwelling Presence, the Spirit of fear. He gave us a Spirit of love, power, and a sound mind. And what is this "power"? It actually refers to power that is authentic authority. In Matthew 28:18, when Jesus said, "All authority has been given to Me in Heaven and on Earth". He was saying, anything in the realm of Divine authority is His. In turn, God has given us an authority based upon His. We actually can refute Satan. We can address him, in the authority of Christ, refusing to fold in the face of his temptation or his intimidation. As a believer, God has not instilled in you a spirit of fear, but He has given you the spirit of love and a level head. If you want to speak the language of encouragement, you need to speak it with authority, instilling the same godly authority in the minds of those beset by fear. Christians can love when there is nothing lovely about it. By the indwelling Holy Spirit, we have the capacity to think things through and come to God-like conclusions. The Bible says, "We have the mind of Christ" (1 Corinthians 2:16). By the indwelling Holy Spirit we actually can think after the thoughts of God; we can actually exercise a Christ-like mind.

When thinking about the chemistry of discouragement, we must not overlook the ingredient of anger. When we are angry, and bitter, we are led to discouragement's front door. As long as anger is allowed to linger, it develops into a root of bitterness. A root of bitterness poisons life beneath the surface and misery sets in. There is no fulfillment in anger, anyway. Have you ever been angry to the point of total satisfaction? Anger just doesn't lead to total satisfaction. You may extract your "pound of flesh", you may get "even", but it doesn't lead to peace.

The consequences of discouragement are as identifiable as its chemistry. Discouragement is not a condition in isolation, it has specific consequences. One outcome of discouragement is misrepresentation. Discouragement leads us to the place that we misrepresent our Lord. We misrepresent ourselves. We misrepresent the spirit of power, love, and a sound mind. In other words, a Christian who is in a state of ongoing discouragement is a Christian who is living out a misrepresentation. I don't like to misrepresent myself, though I have done it. In so doing, I have been ashamed of myself. It is a much more serious thing, however, to misrepresent the name of Jesus Christ, to give people an impression that He is something He is not. To give people the impression that He is angry to the point of wanting a pound of flesh, or that He has a sullen spirit, is to misrepresent Him.

One of the things we particularly need to be careful about is a sarcastic and caustic tongue. Years ago someone told me, "Sarcasm can be the first and the last argument of a fool." Think about that for a moment. If you've got to resort to sarcasm, putting someone in his place because you want to belittle him, the problem is yours not his. Hardly can misrepresenting the grace of Jesus make you feel better!

Still another consequence of discouragement is <u>distrust</u>. You can get so discouraged, or have been discouraged so long that you hardly trust anyone. You can't put your weight down on disillusionment or disappointment any longer, and distrust sets in. Distrust destroys marriage. Distrust threatens relationships between parents and children. It ruins friendships. It greatly affects relationships within the life of the church. Distrust, left unaddressed, translates to bitterness and retaliation. To say the least, distrust is the slippery slope of discouragement!

Discouragement not only spawns distrust, it leads to <u>intimidation</u>. When we are intimidated and fearful, we can settle for a weak conclusion like, "that is just the way I am". Now we are back to being a misrepresentation. Intimidation is not a Christ-like mentality. If Christians take Christ-likeness seriously, to be intimidated is to misrepresent the spirit of Him who gives us power, love, and a sound mind!

When discouragement runs its uninterrupted course, it culminates in debilitation and depression. Are you acquainted with anyone who lives a life constantly surrounded by dark clouds of depression? Starved for encouragement, thirsting for affirmation, a person senses no reason to live. Along the way, to have heard some voices of encouragement could have made the difference.

On that note we would do well to turn our focus on the <u>conduits</u> of encouragement. And what are the conduits of encouragement? What brings on encouragement? First of all, it is <u>simple history</u>. Remember what the leaders of the synagogue said to Paul and Barnabas? "If you've got any word of encouragement, if you've got anything for us, please say it" (Acts 13:15, author's paraphrase). And so Paul begins with what? Simple history. If you really want to be encouraged, think about what God has done before! Over and over again we have to realize history speaks for itself. Has God been there for you in the past? Yes. Has He been there for you when you were discouraged? Yes. Has He been there for you when you were broken? Yes. Has He been there for you when you were lonely? Yes. He said, "I will never leave you, I will never forsake you" (Hebrews 13:5). Does not history bear that out? Simple history is a chief source of encouragement. God keeps His word. His faithful record speaks for itself.

Not only simple history, but <u>complete forgiveness</u> generates encouragement. There is neither real peace, nor much encouragement for life until or unless we can accept the fact that God has forgiven us. I've had my own tussles with that. I have struggled with how undeserving of forgiveness I am. Satan leaps to his opportunity and punctuates my doubt. Discouragement sets in. Guilt multiplies. Only a revisitation of God's grace can transform the moment. Happily, when we accept God's forgiveness we're in a better position to reason, "If He can forgive me, I must be able to forgive others." Often we are reminded, as we approach an observance of the Lord's Supper, we cannot truly celebrate God's forgiveness if we withhold forgiveness from someone else. The Bible speaks about the danger of partaking of the symbols of God's grace while refusing to be gracious and forgiving to someone else. To be complete, forgiveness is both received and given, making possible the encouragement of a clear conscience.

The role of <u>verbal affirmation</u> is huge in offering encouragement. Simply to acknowledge someone's presence can add to their sense of self-worth. A timely compliment, even an honest criticism, can do wonders in the realm of confidence. By the same token, an exaggerated compliment or an excessive criticism can do unnecessary damage to someone's esteem. A Christian, speaking or writing affirmations, can be an effective witness at the workplace, the church house, and at home. Apologies, gratitude, simple courtesy, along with a spontaneous, "I love you," become credentials for soul winners, disciplers, and encouragers.

We have clear instruction from Paul's letter to the Colossians: "Let your speech always be with grace, as though seasoned with salt, so that you will know how you should respond to each other" (Colossians 4:6). Take it from a slow learning father of three boys; it takes a hundred "at-a-boys" to balance one criticism. Verbal affirmation is a vital part of the language spoken by tongues of encouragement.

What Paul and Barnabas were asked to do was to offer hope to a needy congregation in Antioch. Literally, they were asked to say something that would "stand along beside" those people who needed <u>loving companionship</u>. So the word of encouragement Paul gave then had to do with the Paraclete, the Holy Spirit, the One assigned to be both with us and in us. Therein is the underlying encouragement: With the Holy Spirit in me, and beside me, I have resources beyond my own to respond at levels beyond my reach.

Numerous times, over the years, I have had people ask that I go with them to surgery, or to court, or to face a challenge. I was not to be the surgeon, the attorney, or the spokesperson. I was to simply be someone who cared enough to be at their side.

One of my sons leads an international mission's ministry under the title, "Answering The Call". During the last few years, he has secured property just below the rain forest in western Costa Rica. Now that property has been developed into a retreat and conference center, known as Refugio Solte. The Spanish meaning of that name clearly defines the purpose of the center; it is a refuge of release, a harbor of hope, "an R and R" (rest and relaxation). One of the chief purposes of Refugio Solte is to provide international pastors, serving in dangerous and exhausting ministries, a place to spend the time needed to rest, heal, and regain strength for spiritual warfare. Simply stated, Refugio Solte was built and is operated to be a surrounding of encouragement. You could say it is a place where the vocabulary of encouragement is fluently spoken every hour of every day.

As believers, we could revolutionize our own impact upon others if we saw ourselves as a personified Refugio Solte, having learned to come along beside those who are hurt and hopeless, speaking with gentle authority the language of encouragement.

> "Careless seems the great Avenger;
> History's pages but record,
> One death-grapple in the darkness,
> Twixt old systems and the Word;
> Truth forever on the scaffold,
> Wrong forever on the throne.
> Yet that scaffold sways the future,
> and behind the dim unknown,
> Standeth God within the shadow,
> Keeping watch above His own."

-from The Present Crisis, 1845
James Russell Lowell,
Masterpieces of Religious Verse,
(Harper and Brothers, 1948), 118

Chapter 8

The Silent Tongue

"Even a fool, when he holds his peace is counted wise" (Proverbs 17:28).

It seems many of us have kind of a love-hate relationship with people who talk a lot. We are not especially attracted to people whose mouths are locked in at cruising speed and who dominate practically every conversation. We make jokes about people who are long-winded; particularly those who do most of their talking from the pulpit. Yet, at the same time, we have a strange attraction for people who have what is called the quick mouth, the fast tongue; those who know how to turn a phrase; who know how to coin words; those who know the rhetoric and slang of the moment. But we ought to be very careful how we so quickly label people as being sharp or courageous because of how they talk, or how long they talk, or how loud they talk. Because the fact of the matter is some of the most insightful, most penetrating and courageous people you will ever meet are comparatively quiet people. They do not have a great deal to say; but when they speak, you ought to listen. Be careful not to label someone as being brilliant just because they know how to turn a word or coin a phrase.

The Scripture speaks effectively about the right use and the wrong use of the tongue. It is amazing how many times the Bible addresses that subject. For instance in Proverbs 17:27-28, we have a very interesting description of the appropriate and inappropriate use of the tongue. Solomon is led to write, "He who restrains his words has knowledge and he who has a cool spirit is a man of understanding. Even a fool, when he keeps silent, is considered wise. (That's interesting, if you keep your mouth shut, if you're bright or not, no one will <u>know</u>!) When he closes his lips, he is considered prudent." I guess next to Scripture passages like this one; the old anonymous adage says it about as well as it can be said: "There are times when silence is golden. And there are times when it is just plain yellow." There are other moments when to speak is unwise and serves only to confuse. And there are moments to speak because the situation calls for it and requires the courage of our convictions. There are moments when people want us to speak the courage of <u>their</u> convictions! For us there is the need to know the difference; to know the moment; to read the situation. God's people, in some instances, need to speak and other instances we make a far better witness and greater impact if we hold our peace.

There are some simple guidelines for us to consider about when to speak and when not. These guidelines determine when the silent tongue is appropriate and when it's not. First, it is best that we keep our silence, <u>when there is a rumor not to be perpetuated</u>. In James 3:5, there is a graphic description of what a great matter a little fire kindles. Destructive wild fires can be caused by a tiny spark. That's descriptive of the spark of gossip. What anguish and damage can be done because of a tiny spark of rumor that hits the right place at the wrong time! It is reasonable to ask, have we ever made this matter of gossip a matter of prayer, really. I wonder if it might not be a good thing if we would simply learn how to pray something like this: "Father, make me one of those people who is responsible for breaking the rumor chain." The term often accorded to people who put an end to something is "a buster". Can you hear yourself praying, "Lord make me a gossip buster"? Or, Lord make me a genuine saboteur of the rumor mill; make me one who is responsible for bringing the whole enterprise to a grinding halt." What a prayer, "Lord make me a genuine saboteur of the rumor mill!"

There is another time and place wherein God's people would do well to be silent. That's <u>when there is an enemy not to be encouraged</u>. In Paul's letter to the Christians in Rome, he addressed the issue of responding to their personal enemies. He admonished them:

> "Never pay back evil for evil to anyone. Respect what is right in the sight of all men. If possible, so far as it depends on you, be at peace with all men" (Romans 12:17-18).

Now recognize to whom he's speaking; he's speaking to Christians. Non-Christians would not find this to be instructive. In fact, non-Christians, or those who live in shallow spiritual waters, would find the instruction to be just a bit ridiculous. In fact, they probably would be inclined to be cynical about it; so take stock of your own reaction.

> "Never take your own revenge, beloved, but leave room for the wrath of God, for it is written, 'Vengeance is mine; I will repay', says the Lord. But if your enemy is hungry, feed him and if he is thirsty, give him drink; for in doing so you will heap burning coals on his head" (Romans 12:19-21).

In other words, do the unexpected. To state it simply, if you do what everyone else does, you encourage the enemy. Your enemy can feel justified in whatever he is doing to you. However, if you return to him the unexpected he is stymied and the search light of guilt is put upon him. A time to be silent is when there is an enemy not to be encouraged.

Third, a time to hold your peace is when <u>there is a truth not to be squandered</u>. I am intrigued with the number of times in the Bible when the Lord instructed his disciples not to tell anyone what they had witnessed. It might have been a miracle, an astounding event to which they were exposed and he told them to keep it to themselves. For instance, coming down from the Mount of Transfiguration He told His disciples to resist the excitement of recounting what they saw there. Why? Does that seem reasonable? Well, it's obvious He was teaching those disciples to avoid relating things to people who are incapable of appreciating what they are told. In effect, He told them not to squander something that is rich and dear to them on someone who cannot appreciate it. He put it very bluntly in Matthew 7:6: "Do not give what is Holy to dogs and do not throw your pearls before swine, or they will trample them under their feet and turn and tear you to pieces." What is He saying? Don't put pearls out for swine to eat; they don't know how to appreciate it. If you put pearls before them, they'll devour them and turn about and wipe their snouts on your pant legs! That's a loose translation, I know, but it's what He means.

Don't squander truth. There are some people who cannot possibly appreciate it. Television evangelist, Oral Roberts once said he was going to return to earth and would rule and reign here. Some of the media picked up on that and dealt with the man as if he was mentally irresponsible. If you know your Bible, you know it says that, "when the Lord returns to this Earth to lay claim to it, those who have died in the Lord will return with Him and will share in that glorious claim of this Earth in the reign of Christ" (Revelation 20:6, author's interpretation). That was the event to which Mr. Roberts was making reference. But those who do not know and understand Scripture would deem the statement irresponsible and worthy of ridicule.

Comedian Jackie Gleason died at age 71. He was a successful entertainer for years. Of his own admission he led a rampant life style. He drank heavily. He was a chain smoker. He once was asked if he thought when he died he was going to Heaven. Reportedly, Gleason said, "Not if they are real strict about the rules".... "I just hope God has a sense of humor." Well now, that's funny, I suppose, in the comedian's context, but people who take the Bible seriously find difficulty with the idea that God deals with eternal destinies on the basis of His sense of humor. But that's an example of being unable to comprehend profound scriptural truth without trivializing it. Jesus said it is better to hold your peace than to squander truth with those who do not know to respect it.

It is time to be quiet <u>when there is a confidence not to be broken</u>. This is one of those areas where you need to be prepared to pay a price. Those who are in positions of confidentiality, who deal with counseling situations, are often confronted with an unmistakable awkwardness. Because you have been told of sins and failures and have kept the confidence of that information, later on, the person who confided in you can resent you, even turn against you. You just know too much. Be that as it may, confidences promised must be confidences kept. Thin line though it is, however, we cannot promise to keep confidential that which will endanger the life of another person. There are times when ministers will use a life situation as a sermon illustration and people will assume he's breaking a confidence even though he does not mention names or other telling details. It makes for sticky circumstances, but the best rule of thumb is if you are given a confidence you maintain it with your silence.

Lastly, <u>when there is a temper not to be indulged</u> is still another time to hold our peace. The Bible says that God gets angry, why can't we? The Bible does say God gets angry (Psalm 90: 7, 11). Notice, however, what else the Bible says about God's anger. The Bible says God is <u>slow to anger</u>. Yes, God becomes angry. There are moments when his indignation is righteous. There are moments when there is injustice and God unleashes His anger. But God is, by nature, slow to anger. My problem is that I'm quick to it. That's probably your problem. Our tempers have short fuses. This is where we would do well to remember the Scripture's admonition wherein we are told, "A gentle answer turns away wrath" (Proverbs 15:1). We are told, "Be angry and yet do not sin" (Ephesians 4:26). Colossians 3:8 tells us we are to put off anger like you would put off old clothes when God gives you a new wardrobe in redemption. Bottom line, keep your silence when there is a temper begging to be indulged.

Just as there are times to hold our peace, there are times when God's people need to speak up and speak out. A silent tongue is inappropriate in these situations. For instance, God's people should speak, indeed, <u>when there is a Savior to be acknowledged</u>. When the redeemed of the Lord are to say so, they should, indeed, say so. That is one reason why I feel so comfortable with an altar call or invitation during a worship service. The Scripture clearly teaches in Romans 10:10-11, "For with the heart a person believes, resulting in righteousness, and with the mouth he confesses, resulting in salvation. For the Scripture says, whoever believes in Him will not be disappointed." And so when you publicly acknowledge Christ, when you openly acknowledge Him, you make a statement that is declarative to the world, that you belong to Him and His people.

When conversational opportunities arise wherein we can identify ourselves as believers in Christ, we should avoid sounds of pride and exclusiveness in our identification with Jesus and His Church. In fact, the spirit of humility and gratitude are best companions to our confessions of Christ.

God's people also need to speak <u>when there is a witness to be shared</u>. My favorite of all passages in the Bible about a witnessing situation is not in the New Testament. Interestingly enough it is in the Old Testament. In 2 Kings 7:3-11, there is a passage about the four leprous men who sat at the entering in of the gate and begged from those who came by. There was a drought in the land and these men were starving. They finally came to the conclusion that the best thing for them to do was simply go and find the enemy, the Arameans, and give themselves up. They realized they would be prisoners of war, but at least they would have something to eat. So they went to the Aramean camp to give themselves up only to find that God had created a disturbance like unto an earthquake and the enemy had fled the camp. The Arameans left behind their food, their clothes, gold, silver and spoils of battle. These four leprous men went into the abandoned camp and began to eat, to collect clothes, gold and silver. Suddenly they said, "We are not doing right. This is a day of good news but we are keeping silent. Let's go and tell the king's household." (author's paraphrase) I think that passage is beautifully applicable to us as Christians. We've come to know the joy of the Lord, His forgiveness, and we know what it is to be named in the family of God. If we hold our peace we do not a good thing, because these are days of glad tidings. We need to tell others.

A church member once told me about a working associate who came to him for advice. He realized it was an opportunity to witness to his friend about Jesus but he found it difficult, having never done it before. After that opportunity he talked the matter over with his wife and the two of them prayed about it. They said, "Lord if you'll give either of us another chance we will not fail to share Jesus." Sure enough, the Lord did give another chance in a matter of just a short while. Afterward my friend said, "I can't tell you how exciting it was to discover that I can use my tongue as a witness for Christ." Have you made that discovery yet? I yearn for you to make it, because some of you have not made that discovery. Some Christians live under the intimidation of embarrassing themselves or embarrassing someone else. We need to claim the liberty of speaking naturally of Christ as we speak naturally of other things. You don't hold your peace; you don't hold your silence, when you have good tidings to share.

Obviously, God's people need to speak <u>when there is a church to be strengthened</u>. And just how do you strengthen a church? I have five very quick suggestions.

1. You join it. That's a statement, you see, just like we said a moment ago. When you publicly acknowledge the fact that you have received Christ and you become part of a church you make a statement. The statement is: I am a part of this fellowship; I'm a part of its growth. I'm a part of its desire to grow. I'm part of its strength; I'm a part of all that it is.

2. What else do you do to strengthen a church? You attend it. Every now and then someone will say, meaning well, "I'll be with you in spirit." That doesn't even build up the Invisible Church; much less the visible.

3. We need to give to God's church. If you believe that your church is committed to a ministry that is on the right path, then you need to support it. You need to be a financial, consistent, supporter of the life of that fellowship. That's your portion in helping to encourage the body.

4. We need to pray …. For healing, comfort, affirmation, forgiveness within the church and for courage and vision as the Church penetrates the world around it.

5. We need to communicate to the church. That communication needs to be spoken, written, timely and

positive. Even when we are communicating about our failures, the tone should be positive. In 44 years as a pastor, I was renewed and affirmed often by notes like these: "Pastor, I can't tell you how many Sundays I've composed this note and by Monday morning it was forgotten. Not this time. I know you receive many notes, many letters, and they contain profound thoughts. There are no such profound thoughts in this one. I simply want you to know how much I appreciate and love you as my shepherd and my brother in Christ." Oh, but there are some profound thoughts in that letter. It's the profundity of encouragement, of affirmation. Then there was this note, "Dear Pastor, It has not been an easy year. But God has been very good to us. And He's helped us through the things that have seemed insurmountable. We feel God has used our church family in a tender and loving way to lead us beyond these difficult times. As a result we now know Him in a special way. We want to make a special gift over and above regular giving as a way of thanking the Lord. Without His guidance we know our lives would not have the meaning they do today." And with the note was a check for $1000 dollars. When you communicate verbally, visually and reciprocally, you are God's merchant of encouragement to His people.

We need not have a silent tongue <u>when there is an evil to be opposed</u>. We live in a great country. I love being an American. But there are things in our nation that need to be set right. There are injustices. There are immoralities. There are winnable moral and ethical wars for us to wage. There are Letters to the Editor to be written. There are legislative proposals to be supported and there are proposals to be opposed. There are ballots to be cast and public officials to be prayed for. There are even political opponents to be prayed for. The Bible reminds us that God can change the minds of Kings. There are fellow believers who seize their platforms to be a witness. They need affirmation not to be forgotten. Clean language, pure choices, unbending convictions all fire their shots in spiritual warfare. There are movies to commend and movies to decry. There is music to enjoy and artists to be appreciated. And there is a whole world of music that should be left in its underworld. God's people need not be silent about the goals of godliness but run the risk of ridicule while insisting there is a right side to be on.... The Lord' side.

We need to speak <u>when there is a hurt to be healed</u>. Hurts are everywhere. Not just among street people, or the disenfranchised. There are wealthy people in this world who are as miserable as the homeless. They are hurting. There are lonely people everywhere to be found. Among the loneliest people in America are college students. According to Suicide.org, a non-profit organization dedicated to the prevention and awareness of suicide, the 2nd leading cause of death among college students, is suicide. There are hurting people everywhere. And God's people should not silence the hope that is in them. There are guilt-ridden people, living in the pain of unforgiven sin. And there are those who have withheld forgiveness for so long they have settled for compartmentalized misery. When we speak with compassion and truth we can make a difference in the hurting world.

It was the final service at a conference where I was preaching. About 1700 people were registered, most being couples and families of church staff members and lay leaders. In concluding my message, I related my experience of ministering to a death row inmate and accompanying him to his execution. Needless to say, in the months I ministered to a condemned man, the subject of forgiveness had to be dealt with, and often. It was a heinous crime the man had committed. He never denied it. With a grubbing axe and in a drunken stupor, the man had bludgeoned his wife and two of three daughters to death. I had to deal with myself over the question, "How can such a murderer ever be forgiven?" Yes, Saul of Tarsus was the forgiven killer whom God used to write two-thirds of the New Testament. So when this man asked Jesus to save him, I affirmed his salvation.

The morning of his execution, the man about to die asked me, "Preacher, when they pull the switch will I be with Jesus?" In such a moment, there can be no equivocation. I looked a forgiven murderer in the eye and said, "Yes, you will."

After relating my experience, I asked the audience to write 3 names on a slip of paper, names of people they desperately needed to forgive. There followed a period of heart searching and decision making.

After the service, numbers of people gathered around to speak with me, among them a mother, her two adult children and their pastor. The mother spoke first, "This has been a difficult night for me. Seven years ago my husband was murdered and I have been unable to forgive his killer. I have been a prisoner to my own vengeance. Tonight, the Lord gave me the grace to forgive and I am a free woman!" Momentarily, her son embraced me and said, "Thank you, thank you, this is the first time in seven years I have had the courage to forgive someone I don't really like!"

Christians have healing in their tongues, waiting to be spoken!

> Then they (four lepers) said to one another,
> "we are not doing right.
> This day is a day of good news,
> but we are keeping silent...
> Now therefore come let us go and tell the kings household."
>
> II Kings 7:9 (NASV)

Chapter 9

The Household Tongue

"And Samuel lay until the morning and opened the doors of the house of the Lord" (I Samuel 3:15).

To be such a good and godly man, the Old Testament priest Eli, experienced heart-breaking disappointment as a father. He had two sons who developed into despicable men. We read this account in 1 Samuel 2:12, "Now the sons of Eli were sons of Belial; they knew not the Lord" (KJV). Bluntly put, but such was the case. So a godly priest experienced the great disappointment of two wicked sons. Eli's voice had blessed and instructed many people over his years, but that same voice, as far as his sons were concerned, was something to which they had turned a deaf ear. We learn Eli had earnestly attempted to capture the attention of his adult sons. He had admonished and pled with them to set their lives right with God. The Scripture says, "Notwithstanding they hearkened not unto the voice of their father, because of that the Lord would slay them" (1 Samuel 2:25, KJV). In other words, the rebellion of Eli's sons qualified them for an early death.

Even though Eli had experienced broken heartedness over his own sons, God allowed him to have influence and impact on someone else's son. That son came to live with him and his name was Samuel. In 1 Samuel 3:1-11, we discover how Samuel came to experience the fatherly influence of Eli. It was Samuel's mother, Hannah, who brought her son to the aging priest and asked him to invest his undivided influence in the boy. "The child Samuel ministered unto the Lord before Eli and the Word of the Lord was precious in those days; there was no open vision" (1Samuel 3:1, KJV). That is not to say the Word of the Lord is not precious at all times, it means that it was all too rare in those days. Furthermore, "visions were infrequent" (NASV). There was a drought as far as the Word of God was concerned. There were those who had no ear for God's Word, therefore it was a rare and a prized commodity.

> "And it came to pass at that time when Eli was laid down in his place, and his eyes began to wax dim and he could not see. And ere the lamp of God went out in the temple of the Lord, where the ark of God was, and Samuel was laid down to sleep. That the Lord called Samuel and he said, here am I. And he ran to Eli and he said here am I, you called me. And he said I did not call you, lie down again. And he went and lay down" (1 Samuel 3:2-5, KJV).

The same scenario was repeated two other times. Finally, both Eli and Samuel recognized it was not Eli calling the young Samuel in the night; it was the Lord God, Himself. We read on:

> "The Lord came, and stood, and called as at other times, Samuel, Samuel. Then Samuel answered, Speak, for your servant hears. And the Lord said to Samuel, Behold I will do a thing in Israel, at which both the ears of every one that hears it shall tingle" (I Samuel 3:10, KJV).

The Lord announced He was going to do something in the sound of the ears of all Israel that would cause them to wake up and listen.

This is a graphic illustration of a basic Biblical truth. In the home, in the relationship between parent and child, there is to be the kind of training and influence whereby the voice of the father prepares the child to hear the voice of the Heavenly Father. It is just that basic; the parents so prepare the child, that when God speaks, the child responds obediently and happily. Eli had met with great disappointment with his own sons. But given the opportunity to impact and influence another person's child, his voice had prepared Samuel for that time when God would speak and Samuel would hear. Not only did Samuel listen, he responded saying, "I'll do precisely what you call upon me to do" (1 Samuel 3:19b, author's paraphrase).

When our family moved to Roanoke, Virginia, we found and bought a home on the outskirts of Roanoke County. At that time there were only three or four other houses on our street and there were a lot of vacant lots, open territory, and woods for our sons to explore. Needless to say the neighborhood has changed a lot. Houses have been built in every direction and we live in a well-populated suburb. In the process, something else has transpired. After 300 mortgage payments, I became a home owner. As I think back across the years wherein I have lived in the same house, I sense certain tones of voice that characterize the memories connected to each room. I remember exchanges of conversation, cross-road decisions, heartaches shared, laughter over antics of children, daily prayer times, life-altering prayer seasons, discipline, apologies, and farewells. From room to room I hear voices, words, tones coming together to form what I shall call the <u>household tongue</u>.

I would like to share with you some observations as I mentally walk through my home of many years. I'm going to lead you through the front hall and after that I would like to take you into our kitchen. From the kitchen I will lead you to the dining room. We will walk into the master bedroom and then, interestingly enough, we will leave the house and go to the driveway. After a few minutes in the driveway, I will ask you to follow me behind the house to the patio.

I want you to step with me first into the front hall. If there is any language or characteristic tone of voice that typifies that front hall, it would be the <u>affectionate tongue</u>. Of course, I have some other memories related to that front hall. I recall our oldest son's first night he drove the family car alone, and was due to be in at a certain time. When he was not home at the precise moment he was due, being the novice father of a teenager, I was in that front hall at the door! Because he was almost ten minutes late, I filled the air in that front hall with the language of a riot act! I soon learned how foolish I was. Wasted anxiety leads to the pain of delivered speech. So much better it would have been that he was commended, not confronted. A fifteen minute grace period would have made for a better front hallway speech.

One of the best memories I have of the front hall are those our sons have; namely, the presence of their mother at the front door. When those boys left to meet the school bus in the morning and when they returned in the afternoon, they could always count on the sight of Mom at the front door. She was wise enough not to embarrass those sons with too much "I love you" talk in sight of the school bus. But her presence spoke volumes of love. The words, "Be careful" in the morning and "How was your day?" in the afternoon translated to "I love you and you are more important in this house than you know." Over the years that front hallway came to represent a home where the language of affection was spoken. So it should be in every home. Don't be afraid of the language of love. Learn to frame the vocabulary of affection. Allow the household tongue to voice genuine, consistent affection. Such is a language that can translate itself.

Now I want to take you into the kitchen. If you were to ask what voice, or language characterizes the kitchen, what would be my answer? I would say it is the <u>authentic tongue</u>. Like many of you I suppose we've done most of our living in the kitchen. I don't know where headquarters is at your house but it's probably the kitchen. For us, the centerpiece is the kitchen table. So, the kitchen is where the day starts. It has been the place of family prayer. It is where notes have been compared, small talk and serious subjects broached. It's also been the site of family conferences. To remember family conferences is to be reminded of lessons learned. Fathers are famous for announcing conferences that are often the quickest way to get everyone in place to proceed with not listening to a single word being spoken. On a well-chosen day, my wife offered some excellent counsel, "Dear, you will communicate a lot more if you will talk about things when <u>they</u> raise the subjects rather than when <u>you</u> raise them." She helped me understand I am better heard when I am caught in the act of being authentic rather than when I mount my bully-pulpit! There are various places to find authentic faith, authentic prayer, authentic opinions, authentic leadership; but more likely than not, authenticity is best found right at home!

From the kitchen I would like to lead you into the dining room. We don't go there very often. It's very special when we go to the dining room, because most of our family meals are shared around the kitchen table and <u>have</u> been across the years. One of the special occasions reserved for the dining room was birthdays. Our sons knew their birthday was a special day. The family went to the dining room. The good silver was out, all of it; as it took all of it for that many place settings. The good china was in place; yes, the good china. The "birthday boy" got to order what he wanted. It's interesting eating a hotdog supper on good china. I noticed that, as the birthdays got older, steak began replacing the hot dogs! And the red birthday plate was reserved for whoever was celebrating the birthday. As I think back on those birthday occasions in the dining room, the language spoken around the table was from an <u>affirmative tongue.</u> Around the house the voice of affirmation is so needed. It's needed not just for children, but with your spouse, your larger family, even guests in your home.

> "It has been said that in a lifetime we have only 25 to 30 close friends, including our immediate family and relatives. They are our earthly network of support when a crisis comes. If we do not

have this network, to whom can we turn and on whom can we rely when a crisis comes?"

From: Jim Henry, *Keeping Life in Perspective*, (Broadman and Holman Publishers, 1996), 126.

From the dining room, we walk through the kitchen again and into the master bedroom. Just to stand in the room is to be flooded with memories. Some of those memories include the sounds of <u>agonizing tongues</u>. Prayer can sometimes be agonizing. There were times when both agony and anxiety were heard in the prayers offered in the bedroom. There was the time our youngest was very sick. A way to stop the internal bleeding was the burden of our prayer. God answered so beautifully by the skillful hands of a surgeon. Agony and anxiety were replaced with celebration and serious gratitude. Through that ordeal an eleven year old became convinced he was to become the doctor he is today.

The agonizing tongue was heard in that bedroom over a couple of teenage sons who opted for rebellion for quite a while. Again, God was faithful to chart them and us through those days, and the sounds of anxiety gave way to tongues of praise. Two loving fathers emerged from that anxious time; one of them is now a minister of the Gospel.

Enormous respect and admiration are lodged into the memory of my wife and mother of those three sons. I have mental pictures of her in the rocking chair that became a significant piece of furniture in the bedroom. I watched her pour over Scripture.

I watched her weep and cling to the promises of God. I heard her speak with a tongue of affirmation, "I love them as they are, looking forward to what the Lord will do to make them into what he wants them to be." What affirmation she brought to my life! What assurance I connect to that bedroom about patience, prayer, hope, family and the many other languages of love and assurance.

Just across the hall from the master bedroom is another bedroom with its own set of memories. I can remember many a night standing at the door of that room, lights out, saying goodnight to a son who was knowingly distant from the Lord. Sometimes I would ask if I could kneel beside his bed and pray. He always agreed to it. Whatever my prayer sounded like to him, there was some agony that echoed in my heart. I prayed for the Lord to have the upper hand in his life. Often, I left the room saying something like, "When the Lord gets hold of your life, you're going to be something else!" It took a long while for that prayer to be answered. When it was answered, God's reply exceeded all my expectations! Unknowingly, I said goodnight so many times to a missionary in the making! My imploring tongue eventually became an overwhelmingly grateful tongue.

For a few moments, I want to lead you back outside, to the driveway. Strange as it may seem, the driveway registers an apology in my memory. The apologetic tongue is connected to a confession, then to a continuing celebration.

It was a typical teenage request: "Can I spend the night with a friend?" As typical was Dad's response, "Yes, but you must stay at the friend's house and go nowhere else." "Yes, sir! Yes sir!" was the response. But there can be a lot hidden in words like, "Yes, sir!" What was hidden in the words, "Yes, sir!" became evident when our telephone rang about 2:30 in the morning. The caller was a county Sheriff's Deputy. Needless to say, four teenagers, riding about in the wee hours of the morning, in a parent's car without permission, had sealed their own fate! The officer assured me he had no problem with my son, but he was in the company of a couple who were a problem. He just wanted me to get my son and take him home. I remember saying, "He may not be in trouble with you, but he is in real trouble with me."

I was angry and rightly so. The ride home was deathly silent. Once in the driveway, and to my shame, there came that moment when I no longer contained my anger. I lost control and the backside of my hand proved it. My temper trumped my character. That incident took place nearly 40 years ago and I remain utterly ashamed.

Looking at this teenager of mine, I said, "Son, I am sorry. I apologize to you. I have every right to be disappointed with you, but I have no right to strike you. You didn't deserve that." I continued, "You deserve what is going to happen tomorrow, but not this outburst of my temper." To this day, he chuckles about the night dad "belted me". Frankly, he was big enough and strong enough then to have taken me on! But I think the reason he and I can remember it with any laughter now is that God gave me the grace that night to apologize. What I did was wrong. But I thank God that in the midst of my failure, God gave me grace to sound the voice of apology. The sound of that voice needs to be heard in every household, and more often than not.

From the driveway I want to take you out to the patio, just for a moment or two. If there is any language typical to that patio, it would be the one spoken by an <u>approachable tongue</u>. That's where we played basketball across the years. The patio eventually developed a couple of large cracks. A new patio has replaced the old one now, but it's the old one with the approachable memories. It seemed to us the old patio basketball court was more important than having our house listed on the Garden Tour. The boys and I played regularly out there. I say played, my sons played; I was just out there with them. They called me "The Klutz". It was always bad news when you got paired with Dad. I was just awkward. I played basketball like I had played football; and that's not the way you play basketball. There was little grace in my movements and I was most always on a collision course with somebody. But what was happening out there on that patio was the making of memories and the development of approachability. And in the process of it all, the patio allowed me still another place to leave an impression with my sons. In all of their lives they never heard a word of profanity in or about their home. Impatient words? Yes. Anger? Yes. Frustration? Yes. Profanity? No. That's a worthy legacy to link to the language of approachability.

To this point, I have led you to those tones of voice and kinds of tongues, that I equate with memories associated with rooms in my house. For purposes of this chapter, they accentuate what I call the "household tongue". Hopefully, the language spoken in our homes helps us to attune to the voice of God. As in the case of Eli, the surrogate father of Samuel, his voice blended with the voice of God! The <u>affectionate tongue</u>, and <u>authentic tongue</u>, and <u>affirmative tongue</u>, and <u>agonizing tongue</u>, an <u>apologetic tongue</u>, and an <u>approachable tongue</u>; all of these tones of voice can definitely make us ready to hear God when He speaks.

I told you about a telephone call at 2:30 in the morning back some years ago. Let me tell you about another one, about the same hour; but, in this instance, a married son was calling. He said, "Dad, I have been trying to go to sleep and I couldn't. I'm wrestling with this thing about what God wants me to do with my life." He continued, "Somehow deep in my heart I sense and feel that God may be calling me to the ministry." Mind you, this was the son about whom another 2:30 AM call was made. He said, "I was lying here talking to God, thinking about all this, and suddenly I thought, if there is one person in the world I can call and ask what it is like when God calls you to the ministry, it would be my Dad." So at 2:30 in the morning in the dark we sat there, miles apart, me on the side of my bed and he on the side of his. And I told him what it was like in my heart when God called me to the ministry. And I guess I'd have to say it was in that moment that I began to realize some of what I've shared with you in this chapter. It is not that you always know what you are doing or is it that you always do the right thing. God knows, I've just told you of times when I did exactly the wrong thing. But I do want you to know that across the years, the voice that you sound and the language you speak in your home makes ready for that moment when God utters His voice and your children know how to respond.

Dr. Charles Fuller

> Never forget the nine most
> important words of any family:
> I love you
> You are beautiful
> Please forgive me

From: *Lists To Live By*,
(Multnomah Publishers, Inc., 2001), 283.

Chapter 10

The Witnessing Tongue

"And now, Lord, behold their threatenings; and grant unto your servants, that with all boldness they may speak your word" (Acts 4:29).

The oft-quoted English Statesman, Samuel Wilberforce, is reported to have said, "Christianity can be condensed into four words; admit, submit, commit, and transmit." If he is quoted correctly, I think he's on to something. <u>Admit</u> that without Jesus Christ you are a lost sinner. You are a sinner by nature and by choice, and without his forgiveness you are without hope, without God, without Heaven. <u>Submit</u> yourself to Jesus Christ as personal Savior, acknowledging that He is the One who died upon the cross, your substitute for sin's consequences. Having died, God raised Him from the dead so that sin and its consequences might be conquered. <u>Commit</u> to Jesus Christ as Lord, that He might by His indwelling Holy Spirit, overrule and motivate your behavior on a day to day basis. In these three of the four words we see that the purpose of redemption is not only the forgiveness of sin, but the molding of a believer into Christ's likeness.

Caught just for a brief time in short-term traffic congestions, I have realized many Christians do not see any relationship whatsoever between being saved and how we drive an automobile. There are still more questions to ask such as, "Do we see a relationship to being saved and how we deal with someone who just rubs us the wrong way?" Is there a distinctiveness about how we handle being overcharged or underpaid? Does our salvation show through how we deal with an irate customer? And when the door is closed at our house, how much of our behavior is a proof text to our testimony? Hear it again. To commit to Jesus Christ as Lord is to invite Him to be in charge of your behavior on a daily basis.

Then we come to the word "<u>transmit</u>". That is, you are to transmit to others, by the words of your mouth, your faith, and your relationship to Jesus Christ. It is intended that by the words of your mouth others might come to know Jesus Christ personally; and be able to have a relationship to Him as Savior.

It was designed from the beginning, and it has not changed, that this world is to be evangelized by word of mouth! Regardless the venue; television, the print media, neighborhood Bible studies, campus evangelism, stadium crusades, personal conversations, the world around us is to be evangelized as we transmit our relationship to Jesus Christ to those we know well, those we just met, or those we cultivate.

Increasingly, we hear it said, "Religion is a private matter. Keep it to yourself. It doesn't belong in the public square." That is a cultural admonition by Secular Humanists, Atheists, Agnostics, and the Devil himself, not from the Bible! We also need the reminder: For this tongue of ours to be a witnessing tongue, means that it is to be disciplined, saturated with love for lost people, and submerged in the power of God's Holy Spirit.

Frankly, some of us are confused about what evangelism is. We enjoy praise and worship times and come away thinking we are spreading the Gospel. We may be encouraging, even discipling, but not winning the lost. There are highly motivated people involved in various causes that are worthy. But that does not evangelize America. Let's say, for instance, we are able to get all of the "right" candidates elected to office; that does not evangelize America. Let's say that we are able to reverse the liberalization of the abortion laws; that does not evangelize America. Let's say that we defeat the lottery; that does not evangelize America. Hear me, all crusaders! You cannot evangelize the nation, politically, or the world, socially. The neighborhood, the town, the country, and the world are evangelized as always, by transmitting one person to another the knowledge of Jesus Christ as Savior and Lord. This world is saved one person at a time, thus the enormous importance of developing Christians who speak with a <u>personal</u> witnessing tongue.

For some keen insights into the nature of a witnessing tongue let's review the events in and around Acts 3 and 4. Following Pentecost, Peter and John, like two good Jewish men, made their way at 3 o'clock in the afternoon to the temple to pray. As they entered the temple to pray they met a man about 40 years of age who had been lame from the time of his birth, who was begging. The beggar asked for a hand out and the Bible records Peter's response, "I do not possess silver and gold, but what I do have I give to you: In the name of Jesus Christ the Nazarene – walk! And seizing him by the right hand, he raised him up; and immediately his feet and ankles were strengthened" (Acts 3:6-7). The man miraculously stood, began walking and started leaping and shouting. The beggar made his way into the temple along with Peter and John and the crowds followed. They gathered at Solomon's Porch, that was right at the corner of the area that was open to the common people. This was where they assembled on a daily basis. In this particular instance they would naturally be curious. This beggar was a virtual landmark at the Temple gate. He had been lame all his life and now he was walking, leaping, and celebrating his healing. These two Jews, now Christians, Peter and John, seemed to be responsible for what had happened. So the crowds gathered around them, full of questions. Suddenly, the Sadducees arrived on the scene.

The Sadducees were the theological and the political liberals in that time. They did not believe in anybody's resurrection, much less Jesus' resurrection. They were the well-to-do and the well-positioned. Very often they cooperated with the Roman military who were occupying that part of the world. They capitulated, working with the Romans to maintain the Hebrew status quo. The Roman Empire was open-minded about a lot of local activity and customs, but one thing they were not open minded about was public disorder. They did not like riots. They did not like public demonstrations; disquiet of any variety. So, where there was anything on the scene that might resemble a riot, the Sadducees were quick to quell it because they did not want anything to jeopardize their deal with the Romans. And when Peter began preaching to the crowd about the resurrection of Jesus, the Sadducees really got into the act! When it was obvious that the crowd wanted to recognize Peter and John as miracle workers, Peter addressed the crowd and lapsed into a powerful sermon:

> "But when Peter saw this, he replied to the people, 'Men of Israel, why are you amazed at this, or why do you gaze at us, as if by our own power or piety we had made him walk? The God of Abraham, Isaac and Jacob, the God of our fathers, has glorified His servant Jesus, the one

whom you delivered and disowned in the presence of Pilate, when he had decided to release Him. But you disowned the Holy and Righteous one and asked for a murderer to be granted to you, but you put to death the Prince of life, the one whom God raised from the dead, a fact to which we are witnesses'" (Acts 3:12-16).

Having heard the sermon, the Sadducees used their arresting power and brought Peter and John before the Sanhedrin. Made up of 71 men, some of the Sanhedrin were Sadducees. The Sanhedrin was somewhat the equivalent of the Jewish Supreme Court. The high court confronted the two men with what they were doing. After all, they were creating a riot, causing a disturbance. In response, Peter made it very plain that he was not going to be in any way intimidated. He was going to continue to preach in the name of the risen Christ. As he continued to bear witness to the resurrection of Jesus, the Sanhedrin immediately jailed Peter and John, holding them for trial. The trial took place the next day before just about every authority in office. In the face of still more threats, Peter continued his speech about Jesus' Saviorhood and Resurrection. More jail time followed, and finally, the two "trouble makers" were released, and instructed not to preach in the name of Jesus any more.

Peter and John left the Sanhedrin, rejoicing that they were even worthy to suffer this kind of censure for the Lord. They made their way immediately to their Christian friends and told them what had happened; how they had been told not to speak anymore in the name of Jesus. That band of believers immediately organized a prayer meeting:

> "When they had been released, they went to their own companions and reported all that the chief priests and the elders had said to them. And when they heard this, they lifted their voices to God with one accord" (Acts 4:23-24a).

Sentences of powerful prayer followed:

> "'And now, Lord, take note of their threats, and grant that Your bondservants may speak Your word with all confidence, while You extend Your hand to heal, and signs and wonders take place through the name of Your holy servant Jesus.' And when they had prayed, the place where they had gathered together was shaken, and they were all filled with the Holy Spirit and began to speak the word of God with boldness" (Acts 4:29-31).

At this point I want you to notice with me the nature and the characteristics of a witnessing tongue; a tongue that speaks out and speaks up concerning Jesus Christ. It is the tongue that has been, remains to be, and shall be until Jesus comes again, the chief instrument by which this world is to be evangelized. If your circle of friends is moved toward almighty God it will be because you and others have the boldness to speak up for

Jesus. If your town is edged toward God it will be because you and other believers have the boldness to use your tongues as witnessing tongues. If anything happens in this nation of ours, whereby it is evangelized and awakened spiritually, it will come because Christian tongues are used boldly in the witness of Christ. And if we have any hope whatsoever of leading this world of approximately 7 billion to Jesus Christ, it will be because we have developed a corporate boldness to speak the common language of a witnessing tongue.

First, note with me that a witnessing tongue is an <u>adventurous tongue</u>. You recall when Peter and John were brought before the Sanhedrin, they were ordered not to speak or teach again, at all, in the name of Jesus. But Peter and John answered them, "Whether is right in the sight in God to give heed to you rather than to God, you be the judge" (Acts 4:19b.) Between the lines these two were saying, "You, who are supposed to be holy men, do you dare to suggest we obey you instead of obeying God? You must answer that question!"

I point out to you, in the face of discouragement; or ostracism or social disapproval; or in the face of awkwardness or our own intimidation; if tongues are ever to be witnessing tongues, we will have to become adventurous in hostile, or near hostile atmospheres. We will have to become adventurous in the neighborhood, at the office, among friends, in social settings, and when asked hard questions. We cannot confine our witnessing tongues to the stained glass world. If they become witnessing tongues, they will have to become adventurous, even as these first century disciples ventured beyond the safe confines of their Christian friends and spoke with boldness in the face of hostility.

A second feature of a witnessing tongue is that it is an <u>authentic tongue</u>. Peter and John said, "For we cannot stop speaking about what we have seen and heard" (Acts 4:20). He was claiming what they had to say was not second-handed or just conjecture. It is very difficult to witness to something you have never experienced. One of the problems we have in the church is that there are too many people who are indefinite about their relationship to Jesus, and being unable to articulate it, they opt for silence. If indeed, we have a personal relationship with Jesus Christ, and we are positive about it, we need not be silenced by any type of intimidation. You can speak certainly because of what you have witnessed, what you have encountered, what you have tasted yourself. The Apostle Paul wrote out what the Holy Spirit had placed on his heart:

> "That if you confess with your mouth Jesus as Lord, and believe in your heart that God raised Him from the dead, you will be saved; for with the heart a person believes, resulting in righteousness, and with the mouth he confesses, resulting in salvation. For the Scripture says, 'whoever believes in Him will not be disappointed'" (Romans 10:9-11).

Jesus was unequivocal, "For whosoever is ashamed of me and my words in this adulterous and sinful generation, the son of Man will also be ashamed of him when He comes in the glory of His Father with the holy angels" (Mark 8:38). A witnessing tongue is adventurous and it is authentic because it speaks of what it knows by experience.

Another quality of the witnessing tongue is that it is an <u>accurate tongue</u>. It cannot afford to be inaccurate; eternities are at stake! Peter had before him an assembled crowd of influential people. This was no time to give the Gospel an uncertain sound. These people needed to be saved, and there is but one Savior! So with an accurate tongue, aflame with passion, Peter spoke:

> "Then Peter, filled with the Holy Spirit, said to them, 'Rulers and elders of the people, if we are on trial today for a benefit done to a sick man, as to how this man has been made well, let it be known to all of you and to all the people of Israel, that by the name of Jesus Christ the Nazarene, whom you crucified, whom God raised from the dead—by this name this man stands here before you in good health. He is the stone which was rejected by you, the builders, but which became the chief corner stone. And there is salvation in no one else; for there is no other name under heaven that has been given among men by which we must be saved'" (Acts 4:8-12).

How's that for accuracy? How's that for pinpointing the facts? Jesus Christ whom you've rejected, now raised from the dead, is the very corner stone of the faith. There is no other name whereby we may be saved but the name, Jesus! It's a dangerous thing to cast about inaccuracies concerning the Lord Jesus Christ. It can be blasphemous. If you don't know Jesus, it's best that you say nothing. But if you do know Him, see to it that what you say about Him is Biblically accurate. A witnessing tongue is adventurous, it is authentic, and it is also accurate.

Something else we learn about a witnessing tongue; it is an <u>accentuated tongue</u> as well. As Acts 4 further unfolds, we find Peter and John with their Christian friends praying, and what a powerful time of prayer they share! The place was shaken where they were assembled; they were filled with the Holy Spirit and found a boldness to speak God's Word. It was not simply a matter of them doing the speaking, or of them speaking accurately; their tongues were accentuated by the power of the Holy Spirit. What a reminder to us! Regardless how accurate you or I may be, regardless how desirous we may be in sharing our faith, it will not be effective lest it is accentuated by the boldness of the Holy Spirit. Even those who are adversarial and do not comprehend what is transpiring, recognize something inexplicable is taking place when God's hand is on it.

> "When they had threatened them further, they let them go (finding no basis on which to punish them) on account of the people, because they were all glorifying God for what had happened" (Acts 4:21).

The witnessing tongue is adventurous, it is authentic, it is accurate, it is accentuated; also it is <u>affirmed</u>. God vindicates, verifies, and uses the witnessing tongue.

"And with great power the apostles were giving testimony to the resurrection of the Lord Jesus, and abundant grace was upon them all" (Acts 4:33). No question about it; there are indisputable results from witnessing tongues accentuated by the power of the Holy Spirit.

There are two sides to the equation of Proverbs 18:21, "Death and life are in the power of the tongue." The tongue can set a terrible fire of destruction or it can start a flame leading to revival and salvation. In the one case, the tongue can gossip bad news or it can be part of the Good News grapevine. In the Bible, the word translated "preach" is, "euangelizo", meaning to bring good news. It is the word from which we derive "evangelism, evangelist". Simply stated, it means "to spread Good News". And in fact, that is what the Gospel is, good news.

> "For whoever will call on the name of the Lord will be saved. How then will they believe in Him whom they have not heard? And how will they hear without a preacher? How will they preach unless they are sent? Just as it is written, 'how beautiful are the feet of those who bring good news of good things'" (Romans 10:13-15)!

It is astounding how the Gospel can be spread, even in the face of obstructions, when God's people simply become gossips of the Gospel.

A few years ago I heard a missionary update about the evangelical church in China. It was said after one hundred years of evangelical missions in China, there were approximately a million Christians. When Mao Tse-tung and his compatriots moved on China to take it over for the Communist Party, the first thing they did was to drive out the missionaries. But the church grew. Next, the Communists removed the pastors. They jailed many of them, persecuted others, some lost their lives. The church moved on. The government then closed the churches, and the church went underground. And the evangelical church still grew. So the communist authorities did everything they could to destroy the Bible, confiscating as many copies as possible. That was probably the greatest mistake the authorities made because evangelicals began memorizing the Bible realizing they were losing it. Since they were not permitted to reproduce it, they begin to tuck away in their minds enormous portions of scripture. Some even memorized virtually the entire New Testament. After Mao's regime, though limited, China opened again. The amazing thing is that the evangelical church in China today, much of it still underground, reports numbers in the multiplied millions. That is one of many amazing stories about the power of the witnessing tongue.

There is another amazing story to tell; at least it is amazing to me.

The Awesome Power of the Tongue

My room was #102 in Memorial hall at the military high school I attended. It was November, during my senior year. As a commissioned officer, I had a private room. It was just before taps sounded lights out, and a knock sounded on my door.

Standing at rigid attention, there stood a private in my company, asking to speak with me, "Sir!" "Stand at ease," I replied. The private continued, "May I talk with you about a personal matter? Sir!" "Sure," was my answer. Still other questions came, "May I call you by your first name? Sir!" My curiosity was up by then and I said, "Sure."

Haltingly, the young man asked, "Charlie, are you a Christian?" I was disarmed, but honest, "I guess not, I'm not sure." Then came the difference-maker, "Do you know how to become one?" By this time his sincerity had me in the palm of his hand, and I answered, "Yes, I do. My mom is a Christian and she has told me about it, and prayed for me."

"Good," my visitor said as he snapped back to attention. "I've just been praying for you the last couple of weeks that you would be saved. Good night, Sir!" With an about-face, he left my room and left me with some unfinished, eternal business.

Sleep wouldn't come, so about midnight, from my bunk, in the pitch dark, I did business with God. If never before, I was certain then I had received Jesus as my personal Savior.

As I write these lines, it was over 60 years ago that I had that life altering experience. God used the courageous, witnessing tongue of a 16 year old to transform my life!

What awesome power is in the witnessing tongue!

Dr. Charles Fuller

> O for a thousand tongues to sing
> My great Redeemer's praise,
> The glories of my God and King,
> The triumphs of His grace!
>
> Hear Him, ye deaf;
> His praise, ye dumb,
> Your loosened tongues employ;
> Ye blind, behold your Savior come;
> And leap, ye lame, for joy!

Charles Wesley
"For The Anniversary of One's Conversion", 1739
Hymns of our Faith,
compiled by William Jensen Reynolds
(Nashville, Broadman Press, 1964), 138

Chapter 11

The Tongue and the Heart

"A good man out of the good treasure of the heart brings forth good things" (Matthew 12:35).

The Awesome Power of the Tongue

When the Bible calls upon us to do business with God it so often tells us to get our hearts involved in the matter. But, when the Bible speaks about involving the heart with God, it is certainly not speaking about that indispensable muscle that is imbedded in the chest cavity and beats for twenty-four hours a day, causing blood to move through our body system. When the Bible speaks about the heart it is speaking about the inmost person. It's talking about where the will is exercised. It is describing that part of you that is the real you. In your heart there is no pretense; it is where you are honest with God. It is where you make those decisions that the outward life lives out. So when the Bible calls upon us to get the heart right with God, it's talking about bringing the deepest self, the inmost you, the real you, in harmony with the Lord. That is precisely why the Bible says of God, "God sees not as man sees, for man looks at the outer appearance but the Lord looks at the heart" (1 Samuel 16:7). And that is why we place focus on the heart as we talk about the tongue. The fact of the matter is that the condition of the heart has more to do with your choice of words, your tone of voice, and the purpose for which you speak at a given time. When we are describing something that is very sincerely spoken we say something like, "That was spoken from the heart." That's descriptive but everything we say has its birth in the heart. All that we communicate really is determined by what we are behind the speech. So if it's the tongue we want to deal with, we first have to deal with the heart.

The heart speaks many languages. Bitterness is the language of the wounded or angry heart. People who have been hurt can become very bitter. People who are angry at the world, in general, are people who usually have a bitter tongue. Compassion is the language of the sensitive heart. People, who are empathetic and have risen above their hurts, have a capacity for compassion. It's the compassionate heart that makes speech a compassionate speech. Generosity is the language of a grateful heart. Those who are thankful for the things they enjoy in life; their privileges, their health, their relationship with God, are people who are usually generous. Courtesy, in the main, is the language of the secure heart. Persons who are insecure and self-conscious, tend to be turned inward. Therefore they are not given to acts of courtesy or consideration shown to other people. Apology is the language of the forgiven heart. Those of us who know what it is to be forgiven, and are deeply grateful for it, are people who find an apology not too difficult to offer. An unrepentant person, dodging his guilt, can be judgmental, harsh and impatient with those in whom he sees his own failures. The condition of the heart, indeed, chooses to tone of the tongue.

Though we cannot exhaust the list in a single chapter, I want to focus attention on some of the languages we speak based squarely on the condition of the heart. In doing so, we will pitch our tent in Matthew's Gospel and stay there, by and large. In Matthew 6:19-20 we learn some things about the <u>language of selfishness</u>. Selfishness is the language of a <u>greedy heart</u>. The heart that is consumed with greed speaks with a self-centered tongue. Jesus said, "Do not store up for yourselves treasures on earth, where moth and rust destroy, and where thieves break in and steal. But store up for yourselves treasures in heaven, where neither moth nor rust destroys, and where thieves do not break in or steal" (Matthew 6:19). Now verse 21 is the cap stone, the bottom line. "…For where your treasure is, there your heart will be also." Your heart, the real you, is where your will is exercised, where your mind is made up, where you determine your behavior, that is where your treasure is. It's all a matter what your values are. To a large extent, it is a matter of how readily you give away those things that are valuable to you. If we only give away those things that are secondary or unimportant, we have not experienced much in terms of unselfishness. When and if we learn how to give away that which we treasure and value highly we learn something about what it is to be freed from a greedy heart. There are three particular areas where greed can consume us: <u>love</u>, <u>time</u>, and <u>possessions</u>. If our consuming concern is that others love us and that our cravings are met, then we do not know much about what it is to give love away. Self-indulging love has no place to go but toward more greed. And greed is capable of twisting and turning words to get its way. If we give time only to that which is left over, or that which is secondary, we know very little about what it is to treasure time. If our concern about time is only about how available other people are to us, we do not know much about being unselfish with valuable time. If our major interest is how finances can serve us rather than how it can bless God and make a difference among those in need, then we have a problem with greed. A greedy heart, one that is focused on treasures that are self-serving, is a heart that will not produce much in terms of unselfish speech. According to Jesus, what you are, is where your treasure is. Where your heart is most occupied is like a billboard advertising who you really are!

The problem is not with treasuring love, time, and possessions, it is with being obsessed and consumed with them. In the context of Jesus' use of the word, "treasure", the word "obsession" would be its adulteration.

To love with purity is God-like. Loving, being loved, and lovemaking are God-given, but when love turns into lust, greed sets in and greed-gone-bad can eventually lead to hate.

To have ambition for a successful business is motivating, but to sacrifice family time, prayer time, and sleep on the altar of ambition is to succeed at being a failure.

To have enjoyable hobbies, to own your dream car, to afford a home better than your last one, are all worthwhile investments; but to become obsessed with "things" is to lose who you are!

We turn now to the <u>language of sensuality</u>. Sensuality is the language of the <u>impure heart</u>. In Matthew 12, we find Jesus speaking very forcefully to a group of people about their speech:

> "You brood of vipers, how can you, being evil, speak what is good? For the mouth speaks out of that which fills the heart. The good man brings out of his good treasure what is good; and the evil man brings out of his evil treasure (obsession) what is evil. But I tell you that every careless word that people speak, they shall give an accounting for it in the day of judgment. For by your words

you will be justified, and by your words you will be condemned" (Matthew 12:34-37).

By no means is the Bible suggesting that you are condemned or saved; you're lost or redeemed, on the basis of your language. What <u>is</u> being said is that on the condition of your heart you are lost or saved. On the condition of your heart you're redeemed or you're condemned already. But your words <u>reflect</u> the condition of the heart. The person, who is sensual, vulgar, and suggestive, is a person who obviously has a mind that dwells upon such things. So if you want to clean up your speech, you first have to clean up your thought life. The thing upon which your mind dwells will be greatly reflected in what you talk about. What your eyes feast upon, and what you allow your mind to dwell upon, has a great deal to do with what you talk about. There are some people, for instance, who are very indiscriminate about the magazines they read, the internet they watch, and the movies they see. They seem oblivious to the fact that their eyes and mind are like a camera, capturing images! Those images shape thoughts, settle into the heart, and are reflected in one's speech. Your tongue follows the focus of your mind. You become sensual on the basis on how you focus your mind. So then your mouth will be no cleaner than your mind and your speech will be no purer than your eyes:

> "Your eyes are windows into your body. If you open your eyes wide in wonder and belief, your body fills up with light. If you live squinty-eyed in greed and distrust, your body is a dark cellar. If

you pull the blinds on your windows, what a dark life you will have! You can't worship two gods at once. Loving one god, you'll end up hating the other. Adoration of one feeds contempt for the other. You can't worship God and money both" (Matthew 6:22-24, The Message).

An <u>irreverent heart</u> speaks the <u>language of sarcasm and exaggeration</u>. In Matthew 9, we find Jesus healing a man who was paralyzed and trembling. Seeing the faith of the person He healed, Jesus said, "Take courage, son; your sins are forgiven" (Matthew 9:2b). Now the people who are Jesus' enemies don't care for Him to start with, and they see in this situation an opportunity to degrade Him. They resort to sarcasm. With careless irreverence, they call Jesus a blasphemer. In reply, verse 4, "And Jesus, knowing their thoughts said, 'Why are you thinking evil in your hearts?'" In effect, Jesus said, "You have belittled me with irreverence. You say I'm a blasphemer. You've dispensed with me through your sarcasm, but I realize your problem is not what you're saying, the problem is you're thinking evil in your hearts. You're not concentrating upon what I am doing or why I'm doing it. You flip aside the credentials of my ministry because you dislike me. There is such evil in your hearts you cannot even celebrate the healing of this man!" There is a thin line between sarcasm and insult. We find certain passages in the Bible where sarcasm is used to pry open doors of denial and naiveté. It is used sometimes to challenge God's enemies. At the same time, we need to admit we are sometimes snide, catty, and devious; caught in the act of ridicule. A person may not be due our respect, but they are due our courtesy. To address disrespectful behavior or errant thinking is one thing, to cut a person down with destructive sarcasm is quite another. Then again, the problem may not be due to our disrespect for others, but due to the lack of self-respect. There are times when we do not have enough self-esteem to function on a higher plain.

Occasionally I receive letters or communications that are written in sarcastic tones. When that happens I am disappointed because the writers tend to represent themselves at a lower stature than they deserve. Not long ago I received a letter from a fellow minister. The whole tone of the letter, from start to finish, was sarcastic. I was disappointed; not for me, but disappointed for him. Frankly, I thought of him as a person of higher stature than that. There is something degrading about any Christian who resorts to being snide, catty, and destructively sarcastic. We are better than that. We have the potential for a reverent, respectful heart. We resort to veiled language primarily because of cowardice. When we speak in oblique and veiled language we probably do not have the courage to say what we really want to say. The question we need to ask is, why sarcasm? What is the point?

The <u>uncommitted heart</u> speaks the <u>language of shallowness</u>. Matthew has a passage in his Gospel about reverence and worship related to speech. "You hypocrites, rightly did Isaiah prophesy of you: 'This people honors me with their lips but their heart is far away from me. But in vain do they worship me, teaching as doctrines the precepts of men'" (Matthew 15:7-9).

In summary, what Jesus said was that there are those who are basically, fundamentally, concerned about the measurements and the opinions of their fellow men. Their mouths, their lips, pass through the motions of worship, but their hearts are far from the Lord. If what you are, in the religious setting, has nothing to do with who you are on Tuesdays, Thursdays, and Saturdays, obviously you have a problem. There is a shallowness concerning your commitment. If we can speak in reverent tones so long as the atmosphere is a "stained glass" one, but we crash in other settings, there is something wrong with the level of our commitment! Jesus says it very plainly; your problem is not that your talk is wrong; the problem is that your talk is right, but your heart is wrong. There is a shallowness; there is a lack of depth. What you are does not produce a behavior that is consistent with what you are saying.

In 2 Chronicles 16:9a, we find: "For the eyes of the Lord move to and fro throughout the earth." God is looking; He is searching, throughout the whole Earth to do what? "That He may strongly support those whose heart is completely His" (2 Chronicles 16:9b). God looks all over the world to show Himself strong in the behalf of those whose <u>heart</u> <u>is</u> <u>perfect</u> toward Him. The word perfect in Scripture refers to wholeness or entirety. It does not refer to sinless perfection, but to maturity. So, the eyes of the Lord run to and fro throughout the Earth to do what? To show Himself strong, to affirm, to give strength to those whose hearts are mature before Him. That's an accurate rendition: He seeks to show Himself strong to those who are <u>not</u> <u>playing games with Him</u>.

Still another language that originates from the heart is the <u>language of saintliness</u>. That tongue belongs to a <u>teachable heart</u>. Before we go any further, we need to deal with the word "saintliness". Most of us have grown up with a reference to saints, sainthood, or saintliness, that is non-Biblical. Generally speaking, a person who refers to a saint today is talking about a venerated statue in the vestibule of a church. Or they are talking about someone whose memory has been elevated out of the ancient past. That is historical and traditional; it is not Biblical. Biblically, the term "saint" refers to an ordinary Christian. For instance, in 1 & 2 Corinthians Paul is writing to a group of Christians whom he is reprimanding for some of their misbehavior, yet he calls them saints. We hear it frequently said, "I'll tell you one thing, I'm no saint." That rationale is supposed to get us off the hook. We are reducing expectations from ourselves. Then, we point to someone else and say "She's no saint." That is designed to put someone <u>on</u> the hook! In the Biblical context, "saint" means "Christian". So the language that we might call saintliness is ordinary, wholesome, Christian verbiage. People who talk like spiritually healthy Christians are people with a teachable heart. They hunger and thirst after what God has to say and has for us to say. In Matthew 13, we'll find Jesus talking about the parable of the seed and sower. He identifies the seed as God's Word, the Gospel. He describes the sower sowing some seeds by the wayside to be eaten up by the fowls; some seed fell on stony places and having no depth, did not gain rootage; some fell among thorns and those were choked out as the thorns grew up with them. But then He said, "And others fell on the good soil and yielded a crop, some a hundredfold, some sixty, and some thirty" (Matthew 13:8). The parallel passage to this in the Gospel of Luke is even more direct. In Luke 8:11 you'll find the Lord says, "The seed is the Word of God." And then he says this, "But the seed in the good soil, these are the ones who have heard the word in an honest and good heart, and hold it fast, and bear fruit with perseverance" (Luke 8:15). Meaning, those who have hearts that are teachable, like fertile ground, thirst and hunger after what God has to say. And when seed from God is sown in that kind of life, in the good and fertile heart, it will bring forth fruit. Saintliness is the language of the teachable heart.

Sometimes we say when you really want to get to the crux of a matter, or to where the problem really lies, or where the solution is, we say, "Let's get to the heart of the matter." We say that often don't we? Maybe you said it this past week in your workplace. "Let's get to the heart of the matter." Get my sales manager in here, "Let's get to the heart of the matter." Get the children together, "Let's get to the heart of the matter." That's what this portion of the chapter is about. You see, the heart of the matter with regard to your speech, your choice of words, your tone of voice, is the condition of your innermost being, your heart. A heart without Christ has no spiritual life in it. A heart wandering far from God has little life to offer. A heart concerned with bitterness has little to say that is uplifting and encouraging. The condition of the heart has more to do with what we have to say and how we say it than we probably have ever realized.

The Awesome Power of the Tongue

Years ago, I worked two summers as a lifeguard at a Christian conference center. During both summers someone drowned, swimming in the lake during restricted, unguarded hours. Swimming is no longer permitted in that lake; it is considered too dangerous. At its deepest point, the lake measures around sixty feet. One evening, after swimming hours were over, a group of people ventured out to look at the lake. They had been traveling all day. They were hot and tired and had just eaten. One of the group, a young man about sixteen, decided he would sneak in a swim. He dived in the water while friends watched and cheered him on. Suddenly, he cramped and went under water as he struggled. Two or three of his friends tried to reach him to no avail. Others rushed to the assembly dining room looking for the life guards. All seven of the life guards rushed to the lake, and after a brief search, we found the young man under about fourteen feet of water. While we worked to revive him, someone hurried to a phone and called for a doctor. We continued artificial respiration, but got no response. Suddenly, we heard the sound of a car speeding down the dirt road beside the lake. The doctor arrived with the halting sounds of screeching brakes. He bounded out of the car with his bag in hand. He asked us to stand aside and he quickly assessed the situation. I will never forget the sight of the syringe and long needle as the doctor prepared to inject a shot of adrenaline into the young man's chest cavity. Twice, the doctor used that injection, but it was too late. Even such a radical invasion right to the heart could not bring life back. That incident took place many years ago, but the meaning of the phrase took on a vivid memory for me. "Let's get to the heart of the matter!"

Concerning the use of our tongues we need to get to the heart of the matter. Whether we are talking about attitudes, goals, language, ambitions, or values, the heart of the matter is simply this: What is our relationship to Christ? Have we ever established such a relationship? Just how vibrant is that relationship now? Is Jesus Lord of our weekdays? Is He Lord of our private thoughts?

"For the mouth speaks out of that which fills the heart" (Matthew 12:34b).... So said Jesus.

"Thou must be true thyself, If thou the truth wouldst teach;
Thy soul must overflow if thou another's soul wouldst reach!
It needs the overflow of heart to give the lips full speech.
Think truly, and thy thoughts shall thee world's famine feed;
Speak truly, and each word of thine shall be a fruitful seed;
Live truly, and thy life shall be a great and noble creed."

>Horatius Bonar, From Be True,
>*Masterpieces of Religious Verse*
>(Harper and Brothers, 1948), 432

Conclusion

A War of Words

It is often said that spiritual warfare in a Christian's life is a battle for the mind. It is also a battle for the tongue. One of Satan's subtle tactics is to use the mouths of professing Christians to ridicule and nullify the finished work of Christ. If, indeed, we have the Spirit of Christ dwelling in us, what comes from our mouths is to be a witness to the reality of His presence within.

> "After Jesus called the crowd to Him, he said to them, 'hear and understand, it is not what enters into the mouth that defiles the man, but what proceeds out of his mouth, this defiles the man'" (Matthew 15:10-11).

> "…the things that proceed out of the mouth come from the heart and those defile the man. For out of the heart come evil thoughts, murders, adulteries, fornications, thefts, false witness (lies), slanders (gossip). These are the things that defile the man" (Matthew 15:18-20).

In His rumble with Satan after the wilderness experience and baptism, Jesus won that battle with God's words.

> "And the tempter came and said to Him, 'If you are the Son of God, command that these stones become bread.' But he answered and said, 'It is written (Deuteronomy 8:3), Man shall not live by

bread alone but on every word that proceeds out of the mouth of God'" (Matthew 4:4).

In that record of spiritual warfare we learn three lessons in particular:

1. Words mean everything if they are the right words, and especially if they are God's words.
2. Satan must respect God's Word when spoken by God's people because those words are authentic and authoritative.
3. In spiritual warfare, Satan will tuck tail and accept defeat only for a season. He is defeatable but he is relentless.

So it does matter that Christians use words God can bless. It is important that Christians do not speak out of both sides of their mouths. If our language is no cleaner or less foul than that of an unbeliever though Satan tells us we are "blending" with the culture, we are, in fact, camouflaging our Christian identity! And it is absolutely indefensible to discover that a Christian's tongue started the fire that destroyed acres of character and truth!

James cuts to the chase with his probing question:

"From the same mouth come both blessing and cursing. My brethren things ought not to be this way. Does a fountain send out from the same opening both fresh and bitter water? Can

> a fig tree, my brethren, produce olives, or a vine produce figs? Nor can salt water produce fresh" (James 3:10-12).

Neither can a vulgar tongue compromise itself into a godless conversation and, at another time, be an authentic witness of Jesus!

In his 5th chapter, James is still at it, extoling the virtues of a straight forward tongue, insisting that there are some things that remain sacred.

> "But above all, my brethren, do not swear, either by heaven or by earth or with any other oath, but your yes is to be yes, and your no, no, so that you may not fall under judgment" (James 5:12).

Given the cultural atmosphere that we live, particularly in America, it may seem the foregoing paragraphs offer a formula for a prudish Christianity. A prudish Christianity? No. A distinctive Christianity? Yes. There is nothing prudish about honesty, reverence, respect and forthrightness.

We can get so caught up in the cultural moment that we can attend a movie, laced with profanity and vulgarity, only to describe it later as a "good movie with one or two bad words".

The exclamation, "Oh, my God!" has become so commonplace it is predictable in most any moment of surprise or pleasure. An expression of prayer and praise to God has been carelessly adulterated.

Recently, a high school valedictorian was denied her diploma until she submitted a written apology for profanely using the word "hell" in her graduation address. Immediately protests came from every direction condemning such frivolous action. I heard a network news commentator, reporting on the event, ask his audience, "What is wrong with using the word "hell" in a speech? It is an everyday English word"!

Using the word "hell" does not pave the road there. There are more serious words in "hate speech" and character assassination, but the point is that in a war of words, God's people are not to capitulate, compromise and conform. What we say and how we say it helps win the culture war or helps to lose it.

As the preceding chapters have addressed the awesome power of the tongue, we have been brought face to face with various aspects of life wherein our words are difference-makers. An acid tongue can destroy a life while an encouraging tongue can give life. A silent tongue can be an instrument of peace or a refusal to be silent can prevent an evil from going scott free! A truthful tongue is a weapon of freedom but a lying tongue is the chief weapon of the father of all liars. It is with the mouth that confession is made into salvation and a believer's tongue is commissioned to make disciples of the nations. Yes, Solomon said it well, "Death and life are in the power of the tongue" (Proverbs 18:21).

God's Word is still our chief weapon and to lay it down to mingle with the enemy is the choice of a coward not the courageous!

Little can be added to the words Jesus chose to come from His tongue in Mark 8:38:

"For whoever is ashamed of Me and My words in this adulterous and sinful generation, the Son of Man will also be ashamed of him when He comes in the glory of His Father with the holy angels."

About the Author

Dr. Charles G. Fuller was born in Andalusia, Alabama and as a child grew up in West Palm Beach, Florida. He graduated from Fork Union Military Academy, obtained his B.A. degree from the University of Richmond and Master of Divinity degree from Southwestern Baptist Theological Seminary. He holds D.D. degrees from the University of Richmond, Campbell University and Fredericksburg Bible Institute and Seminary.

Dr. Fuller began his pastorate at Pine Street Baptist Church in Richmond, Virginia in 1957 to 1961. In October of 1961, he became the pastor of First Baptist Church, Roanoke, Virginia and remained the pastor for 38 years, until his retirement in October 1999. The many radio listeners and viewers of the television broadcast, <u>God's Minute</u>, spanning nearly three decades, continue to comment on the impact of those daily broadcasts.

Dr. Fuller' name is identified with Southern Baptists through his extensive leadership positions in the past. He is a well-known statesman within the Southern Baptist Convention. He was President of the Virginia Baptist State Convention, Chairman of SBC Radio and Television Commission and Chairman of the

North American Mission Board. Dr. Fuller serves as Chairman of the Board of Directors for Answering The Call, an international missions ministry led by his son, David Fuller.

Dr. Fuller is the Chairman of the Board and President of God's Time Incorporated. God's Time, Inc. is a not-for-profit ministry dedicated to reaching others for Christ and ministering to fellow believers through the ministries and messages of Charles Fuller. After retirement from a long pastoral ministry, Dr. Fuller continues to minister through his preaching, teaching and writing. His extensive 27 year radio broadcast ministry, God's Half Hour, remains on numerous state-side radio stations and on a network of short wave stations throughout the world. Under the egis of God's Time, Inc., Dr. Fuller's sermons are available in CD format through the God's Time website, www.godstimeonline.com.

Twice widowed (Pat & Margaret), Dr. Fuller married Carol Fehlman Fuller, an accomplished pianist in March of 2007. Dr. and Mrs. Fuller are teamed in a ministry of preaching and teaching. The Fullers reside in Roanoke, Virginia, and share a family of 5 children, 12 grandchildren, and 3 great grandchildren.